Assessing Pupils:
a study of policy and practice

Elizabeth Engel Clough and Peter Davis
with
Ray Sumner

NFER-NELSON

Published by The NFER-NELSON Publishing Company Ltd.,
Darville House, 2 Oxford Road East,
Windsor, Berkshire SL4 1DF

First Published 1984
© National Foundation for Educational Research
ISBN 0-7005-0664-0
Code 8176 02 1

Typeset by F.D.Graphics, Fleet, Hampshire

Printed and bound in Great Britain
by Billings & Sons Limited, Worcester.

Distributed in the USA by Humanities Press Inc.,
Atlantic Highlands, New Jersey 07716 USA

Contents

List of Tables

List of Figures

Acknowledgements

The authors thank most warmly the Education Department of the Sheffield City Polytechnic for 'housing' the project during its three years. We owe a great debt of gratitude to the LEA Advisers who served on our Advisory Group. Their hard work and enthusiasm at every stage of the research enabled us to address questions about assessment which practising teachers consider relevant. We thank them wholeheartedly. Many schools welcomed us into their busy lives - we thank all those heads, teachers and pupils who spared time and energy to work with us.

We are grateful to the NFER Statistical Services and to Mr. Peter Smedley for processing the computerized questionnaire data. We also acknowledge help from Mr. Andy Stillman and Mr. Chris Whetton of the NFER who reviewed the report in draft form and from Mrs. Linda Nance who produced the several typescripts so efficiently.

Dr. Elizabeth Engel Clough

Mr. Peter Davis

Dr. Ray Sumner

Foreword

Currently much attention has been focused on external assessment of pupils at 16+. This present research is valuable in that it concentrates on assessment in the middle years, referring specifically to in-school procedures. In recent years we have become increasingly aware of the need for a full picture of the developing child and therefore this study over nine LEAs is timely. The research team, based locally, has collaborated closely with advisers, heads and teachers in these local authorities.

The research has proved to be not only instructive but fascinating. Rather than prescribing procedures it describes current practice, but inevitably there are implications for the improvement of assessment procedures underlying the whole study.

The main lesson seems to be that the purposes of assessment have not been sufficiently clarified, with the result that requirements have not always been fulfilled. This alone, even without the many other interesting and useful findings, makes this report of value. It should prove to be a helpful document for heads and teachers and be of particular concern to departments wishing to review their techniques of assessment.

R. A. Buck ⎫
A. M. Taylor ⎬ (Wakefield LEA)

B. Carlson (Sheffield City Polytechnic)

J. R. Howey (Kirklees LEA)

D. Maxwell-Timmins (Calderdale LEA)

J. K. Newberry (Bradford LEA)

P. Robertshaw (Derbyshire LEA)

P. K. Twist (Barnsley LEA)

G. K. Vaughan (Doncaster LEA)

J. West (Leeds LEA)

B. Wilcox (Sheffield LEA)

Advisory Group: Assessment Procedures in Schools Project

Chapter I

The Research: an Outline

Introduction

This book reports findings from an investigation into the assessment of 11–14-year-old pupils. Our aims were basically two-fold. Firstly, we planned to describe and analyse the existing assessment practices for these pupils in a wide range of schools. Through doing so we hoped to examine the ways in which assessments are used by teachers to guide pupils' learning and to adapt the curriculum. It was, therefore, important to gather data about the less formal day-to-day assessment which is practised routinely in classrooms, as well as more formal kinds, such as school examinations, test batteries etc. Secondly, we aimed to identify criteria for the evaluation of existing good practices in assessment. Descriptions and analyses of examples of good practice could, we believe, be helpful to other teachers in developing their own ideas on assessment.

This study differs from many recent investigations into methods of assessment, most notably in the age range of pupils considered. In much previous research attention was focused on the fourth and fifth years of secondary schooling, where of course assessment is often geared to external examinations. But assessments made in the previous three years may be equally important. This is particularly so of the secondary third year when assessments are linked to decisions about allocation to optional courses. Yet there has been little research on this age group.

This inquiry also involved a variety of research methods, both quantitative and qualitative, which complemented one another. Too often questionnaire studies seem unsatisfactory because the issues investigated are predetermined, and case studies appear to be based on the arbitrary hunches of researchers. Here the broad picture painted by analysis of a fairly large-scale survey was enriched and extended by qualitative investigation of topics, the selection of which was at least partly determined from survey data.

The degree of collaboration between practice and research was also unusual in this project; many of the questions for inquiry were identified by local teachers and advisers, some of whom then cooperated closely in the research. In many cases, as well as being of wider interest and applicability, the research results proved useful to the people taking part.

The project was sited in Sheffield because of an earlier inquiry by the LEA there (Wilcox, 1982), conducted to identify training needs relative to pupil assessment. This research revealed a number of findings which carried clear implications for in-service training provision. For example, less than half of the 162 departments surveyed kept permanent records; in more than a third of departments teachers operated their own assessment schemes, since there was no agreed common procedure for marking or grading work. Any standardization of marks or grades across departments, for reporting or for transfer to a central record system, was found to be very rare indeed. A course based on the findings is now organized by the Sheffield LEA.

Concurrent with this local activity the NFER was aware, through its test advisory services, of a general increase in demand from teachers for more information on the conduct and outcomes of pupil assessments. A proposal was therefore drawn up which attempted to link these concerns; by conducting detailed work within a circumscribed region the intention was to raise issues and propose solutions which could be more generally applicable. In the event, nine LEAs in the North of England agreed to collaborate with the NFER on the project and each nominated an adviser to represent the Authority on an Advisory Group. The members of this group, which met every three months or so, were asked for and gave advice. They effected the vital link between the research team and local schools.

Research which is aimed at bridging the gap between practice and research fails if the report of results is only of interest to a research audience. This account is therefore not a research report (in its frequently-used, narrow sense), but rather a report about the implications of our research findings for heads and other teachers, for LEA advisers and for those concerned with in-service and initial teacher training. We have not included a general review of the literature on assessment practices in schools and references and tables of results have been kept to a minimum. On the recommendation of our Advisory Group we have included the questionnaires in an Appendix because it was suggested that these provide a most useful agenda for schools intending to review assessment policies. A summary of results has been inserted on to these, in order to indicate a global account of responses.

Design of the study

The research was organized in three phases: (A) a survey, (B) a number of case studies of innovation (special studies) and (C) development work with teachers. This book reports on the first two phases only.

(A) The survey

The first phase was conducted by questionnaire at three levels. Decisions about the scope and form of the questionnaires were made after consultation with a number of teachers and with members of our Advisory Group. Quite simply, we asked: what would you like to know about assessment of 11-14-year-olds? Drafts were then piloted in two local schools. In the main study ninety-seven headteachers responded to questions about the assessment policies of their schools. It was clearly necessary to obtain information from teachers, as well as heads, in order to piece together a picture of practice, of how assessments are made and the purposes to which they are put. Our decision to seek information at a further two levels – that corresponding to departmental level in secondary schools and at classroom level – was complicated by the fact that our sample contained ten middle schools. We attempted to design a questionnaire which was applicable not only to departmental heads but also to heads of year in middle schools, indeed to anyone with responsibility for either a particular curricular area or a large group of children. Heads of departments and year groups (n=223) and class teachers (n=460) in twenty-seven of the schools answered questions about practice at departmental (or year group) and classroom levels, thus for some schools we were able to draw up detailed profiles of existing policies and practices. Although a majority of questions were pre-coded for computer analysis, both the headteachers' and the heads of departments' questionnaires contained large numbers of open-ended questions.

The sampling design had to take account of the fact that, within the region, there were eight types of school with children in the 11-14 age range. These varied from middle schools with twelve-year-olds in the top year to comprehensives where pupils entered at 13+ years. A representative sample was drawn randomly from the schools of each type, taking account of the number of year groups and a notional number of departments in different schools falling in the 11-14 age range.

One hundred and twelve headteachers were surveyed, approximately twenty per cent of those in the region. Roughly, a quarter of these schools (n=27) completed the other two questionnaires designed for head of departments and teachers (see Table 1). At these levels the secondary schools contributed proportionately more information, simply as a consequence of size. Though a few schools sent in high returns, the general level of response was even across the sample; the implication is that results tabulated for heads of department and teachers are not heavily biased towards a few high-returning schools.

Table 1: Composition of the sample

Survey level	School type									Total
	5-12 Middle	8-12 Middle	9-13 Middle	10-13 Middle	11+ Comprehensive	12+ Comprehensive	13+ Comprehensive	11+ Grammar	11+ Modern	
Headteacher	2	13	25	2	41	8	16	2	3	112
Head of department and class teachers	0	3	6	1	10	2	4	0	1	27
Total number of schools in the nine LEAs	12	95	167	9	166	34	81	9	13	586

Returns for the headteacher questionnaire were excellent with 97 (87 per cent) completed. Head of department and teacher questionnaires were received from every school in the sub-sample and the response rates for these were approximately 50 per cent (head of department questionnaire 53 per cent, teacher questionnaire 48 per cent). However, the percentage return figures for these levels, based on the number of questionnaires despatched by us rather than distributed in schools, were undoubtedly depressed because headteachers requested more, in some cases considerably more, than they eventually gave out. Since our inquiry related to the 11-14 age range we requested that only teachers involved with that age group answer the questionnaire, but this was not apparently always understood when requirements were estimated at the outset.

Generally, the survey revealed considerable lack of coordination at school and departmental levels. Of course the existence of written policies on assessment (containing perhaps a rationale, details of methods of assessment, systems of grading or marking and procedures for collation), is not an automatic guarantee of a well-thought-out and coordinated approach. Nevertheless, it is perhaps surprising that less than half the schools surveyed had a written assessment policy. Similarly, although most departments had agreed a set of teaching aims, only a minority had drawn up any written departmental policy on assessment. Other survey results, however, were more encouraging. There was, for example, evidence that considerable numbers of teachers used the results of their assessments to review lesson content and teaching methods.

(B) Special studies

The purpose of the special studies was to illustrate examples of good or interesting assessment practices. Topics for special study were selected both by examination of questionnaire returns, particularly of the responses to open-ended questions, and also from suggestions made by Advisory Group members and teachers. Some of these studies concerned aspects of assessment which few schools actually practised, yet in which interest was widely expressed. Pupil profiling schemes, pupil self-assessment, and a well-coordinated scheme for the assessment of pupils at transfer to secondary school all came into this category. Others represented examples of innovative practice. These ranged in scope from, at the local authority level, the implementation of a well-established modern language graded testing programme to, at the level of a single department, the development of a new scheme of assessment based on skills required for public examination work. In all cases, drafts of reports were submitted to the teachers concerned for verification and comment, and appropriate revisions were made.

(C) Development work

The third and final phase of the project was concerned with the development and evaluation of new assessment procedures. Collaborative work with groups of teachers produced new approaches and techniques in such areas as the assessment of 'topic' work and the development of assessment procedures for a process-based course in lower school science. The results of these initiatives have been disseminated locally and some may be published later.

The organization of the book

Throughout the book, where specific schools are referred to, pseudonyms have been used.

The three levels of the survey design – school, department and classroom – are mirrored in the organization of the next three chapters which report findings at these levels. Thus, Chapter 2 deals with issues about assessment which concern the school as a whole, Chapter 3 considers departmental policies and practices and more detailed classroom procedures are examined in Chapter 4. At appropriate points within this structure illustrative examples are interposed from the qualitative study of examples of innovative practice. Issues arising from the research are summarized briefly at the end of each of these three chapters, but in Chapter 5 some of these issues are re-visited and discussion of them is extended. The first three sections in this final chapter draw together questions and problems which have emerged from the study: philosophical, organizational and technical problems relating to assessment. In the discussion, we identify some criteria for the evaluation of good practice. In the last section of Chapter 5, emboldened by the strongest recommendation of advisers and teachers, we make a number of suggestions as to how ideas discussed in the book may translate into practice. Our hope is that this conclusion to the study will be useful, both to individual schools embarking on assessment reviews and to LEA advisers and others responsible for in-service provision. For it is quite clear that much practical guidance from LEAs is necessary if the general dissatisfaction about existing practice is to be harnessed to achieve real improvements in assessment.

Chapter 2

School Assessment Policies

Introduction

The purpose of this chapter is to discuss the issues and concerns about assessment which relate to a school as a whole. It is of course artificial to separate school concerns from those of departments and of individual teachers and pupils. Nevertheless, it is possible to identify broad questions of assessment policy which are the province of the whole school and which frame the details of both policy and practice at departmental and classroom levels. We found considerable difficulty in distinguishing between 'policy' and 'practice'. In theory, practice flows from policy so policies must also be (to some extent) prescriptions for practice, whether or not this is made explicit. In any event, we tried to focus our questions to headteachers on policy-making issues. The sample for the headteacher questionnaire consisted of 70 secondary schools (84 per cent return) and 42 middle schools, 15 of which were deemed primary and 27 secondary (90 per cent return).

In this chapter, as well as survey results, we refer to special studies conducted in three local authorities. They are:

The development of a school assessment policy in an 11+ comprehensive school (Woodvale School).

The introduction of a school grading system in an 11+ comprehensive school (Lambourne School).

Assessment procedures related to transfer to a 13+ comprehensive school (Highfield School).

Written statements of policy

Our survey of headteachers indicated that 42 per cent of middle schools and 51 per cent of secondary schools had written assessment policies for the whole school. Nearly 60 per cent of these had been in operation for fewer than five years. Many heads, at the time of responding, had recently embarked on the development of a school policy. However, one third of all schools in our sample neither had an existing written policy nor were developing one. It is hard to imagine that a school can operate without some kind of implicit policy, even if it be, for example, that no formal assessment should occur at all, or that every child should be examined once a year. The headteachers who claimed to have no written policy, nor to be developing one, went on to answer further items on the questionnaire according to practices currently operating in the school.

Results from the teacher questionnaire tallied well, with 40 per cent reporting that their school had a written policy, although many of these teachers had not actually read it. Perhaps not surprisingly, teachers expressed greater satisfaction with the guidance and help offered by their departmental or year group assessment policies than with the school policies.

It is difficult, from the questionnaire results alone, to build up a picture of existing school assessment policies. Do they specify the purposes of assessment within the school? Do they refer to any general educational principles or to curricular objectives? Do they detail procedures whereby the policy be carried out? We invited heads to enclose assessment documents with their returned questionnaires, examination of which might perhaps indicate answers to these questions. However, only 14 schools sent their documents to us (a third of those with written assessment policies). The majority of these were very simple and in most there was no discussion of underlying assumptions or mention of variations across the curriculum. Compared to the diversity of grading/marking systems reported by heads of departments (see Chapter 3), school systems (at least from this small sample) were easily classified into two kinds: a five-point scale of ability and attainment or a five-point scale of ability together with a similar scale for effort.

In two of these schemes grades were defined by an explicit reference to a balanced distribution, with 10 per cent of the population allocated to top and bottom grades, 50 per cent to an average grade, and the rest to below and above average grades (15 per cent). We found that this assumption of correspondence to 'the normal distribution' of ability within groups of children is a feature which commonly underpins thinking in school assessment. One head explained that 'a normal distribution pattern applies to all subjects in all years'.

An imposition of the normal distribution curve on assessment results of small groups denies the experience of teachers – that the ability range of class or year groups may not follow that pattern. The specially 'good' third year, or the unaccountably 'weak' top set in the second year is discussed in every staffroom. Any group of pupils can be divided into lots of 10 per cent, 15 per cent, 50 per cent, 15 per cent, 10 per cent or whatever. Indeed, it is perfectly legitimate to adopt arbitrary proportions in grade units, provided that scores are spread and indicate identifiable differences in attainment and provided that comparisons are not made between sets or years. But it is misleading to think of such a distribution as 'normal' in the technical sense. Only if the score band widths are related to a deviation from the mean in a specific way (conforming to the normal curve) can the distribution be described as normal.

In our special study at Lambourne School where we spent some time talking to staff, a very simple written statement comprising a common grading system had recently been adopted which was interesting in a number of respects. A five-point A–E grading system operated for all subjects. The grades were based on a balanced distribution, with top and bottom grades each accounting for 15 per cent and the average grade (C) accounting for 30 per cent of the group. Assessments were recorded, however, to include the set or class in which the pupil is taught. So, for example, Set 2/4 Grade A indicates that the pupil is in the top 15 per cent of the second set, where the ability range is divided into four sets. Staff see this system as having two main advantages. Firstly, it allows low-set pupils to achieve A and B grades. Secondly, it should provide parents and others with accurate information and with a realistic assessment of a child's performance. The teachers we talked to were not all of the same opinion about parental understanding of the system, however – some thought that the set code would be misinterpreted, and that parents of pupils with high grades in low sets would develop inflated opinions of their child's abilities.

Interestingly, at this school it was decided to omit effort grades from the system because teachers were unhappy about the subjectivity of judgments made in awarding these grades. The whole question of the ethics and practicability of teacher assessment of a range of pupil attributes (including effort, motivation, integrity, responsibility, reliability, etc.) is a contentious issue in many schools and is referred to at several points in the ensuing account.

There was evidence from the questionnaires that many heads felt that they ought to adopt a more coordinated approach to assessment. For example, when asked what changes were currently under consideration for assessment, one head replied, 'Implementation of much of the subject background to this questionnaire,' and another suggested that what was needed in his school was, 'Rationalization and coordination so as to produce a written statement'.

Several headteachers of middle schools indicated that the absence of a written policy did not imply a disorganized approach. One head explained that the school had:

No formal written policies, but accepted procedures are adopted for maths throughout the school; for English, for sciences and French in the 3rd and 4th years (11+ and 12+),

and another that:

There is no actual written policy, but all staff teaching this year group are involved in assessment throughout the 12+ year preparing for transfer.

In smaller middle schools, apparently, heads feel confident that a coordinated approach can be maintained without the formality of written policy statements.

Purposes of assessment

If some headteachers claim to have a perfectly functional and agreed set of assessment procedures, is there indeed any need for school policies? What are they anyway? Are they distinguishable from sets of procedures; from systems of practice? One important distinction may be the specification in a policy of the purposes to which assessment results are put (though this, in fact, is rarely done). To specify purposes is to turn attention to curricular objectives and, indeed, to the wider educational ideals of the school. To understand this connection is to view assessment as an integral part of teaching and learning, an opinion by no means universally held. One headteacher discussed the need to, 'Guard against the danger that assessment may influence and control curriculum content'.

The assumption here is that such influence is educationally negative. One does, of course, encounter examples of assessment results being used to instigate change for the sake of greater administrative efficiency or elegance, rather than for educational merit. Such changes perhaps reflect a view commonly held in schools – that assessment is a discrete activity (presumably equatable with testing), that it has little to do with day-to-day learning and teaching, but rather with people and influences external to the school. As such it should be kept in its place, and should not be 'allowed' to influence classroom activities.

It is rare to encounter any explicit recognition of the key role of assessment in relating the aims of a school to the way it attempts to implement these aims. At class level this is frequently recognized and practised naturally – teachers make judgments about the success of a lesson by asking the question 'did we achieve what was intended?' At school level the relationship between ideals, objectives, methods and evaluation is often obscure.

Woodvale School is an 11-18 comprehensive, where staff are currently battling with the problem of developing procedures based on a theoretical framework which does recognize these interrelationships. We spent some time in this school, talking to the head and to senior staff in order to describe the on-going development of their assessment policy. We hoped to identify the motivating influences for the initiation of the school-wide review, the criteria for its success to date and the areas which have proved particularly problematic. As with all our special studies, the report is not intended to be prescriptive since procedures are rarely, if ever, directly transferable to other settings. Nevertheless, we think there may be some useful pointers for schools considering a review of assessment policy.

Extracts from a document drawn up by the senior management team of the school are given in Table 2. This outlines the framework within which the development has taken place. It specifies very clearly that assessment should reflect learning and teaching practices in the classroom and that these, in turn, should reflect the aims and objectives of the school, which themselves stem from its general philosophy. To recognize a general theoretical relationship is one thing, actually to work at the processes of relating them in detail is much more difficult and time-consuming.

The development of policy should be viewed against the guidance subsequently offered to staff by the management team as to the purposes of assessment within the school. These are outlined in Table 3.

The stated 'principle' of the school (see Table 2), which emphasizes the needs and qualities of the individual pupil and which mentions social as well as intellectual development, gives some clue as to its general ethos. Certain factors seem likely to have coloured this school's approach to the development of a school assessment

Table 2: Extracts from a document drawn up by the management team of Woodvale School as a framework for a school assessment policy

The assessment structure should ultimately arise from the educational principle of the school which is:

> That the education of a pupil should make full recognition of his individual needs and qualities, and should aim to maximize his social and intellectual development, enabling him to attain his full potential.

The primary concern of the teacher, therefore, is with the individual pupil, as opposed to any generalized group of pupils.

To perform this function adequately, the teacher needs to know his clients as individuals, to identify their strengths, weaknesses, attitudes, values and characteristics, in order to develop appropriate strategies and techniques for fulfilling the requirements of the educational principle.

The assessment procedure should form the final stage in the chain:

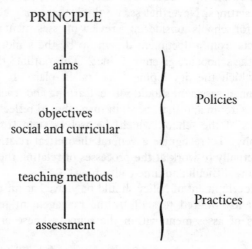

and the procedure should assess the degree of success in meeting the requirements of all four previous stages.

Table 3: Purposes of assessment at Woodvale School

(a)	Instruments for measuring the attainment of the pupil – with a view to introducing suitable remedial action where necessary.
(b)	Instruments to facilitate self-criticism on the part of the teacher with a view to modifying their own teaching methods and strategies where necessary.
(c)	A means of passing on information to a third party, whether it be other teachers within the school, parents or prospective employers.

policy. The school generally emphasizes the education of the whole child and the guidance and counselling system is well developed. Much of the teaching is in groups of mixed ability, though there are departmental variations. One of the assistant heads has responsibility for curriculum development and assessment within the school. There is also a tradition of school-based in-service teacher education, with attendance at courses which have a common theme for a year.

The decision to embark on a school-wide review of assessment was motivated initially, in the words of the headteacher:

By the need to make sense of a jumble of assessment procedures operating in the school at the time and the need to achieve a more unified policy.

Later on in the process they recognized the inadequacy of their old system to provide parents, employers and other agencies outside the school with comprehensive, accurate reports of pupils' achievement and progress. A good school profile, according to a paper produced by the management team, should:

...paint a picture of an individual pupil from many angles that can be readily understood by any member of the teaching staff. The information contained therein should enable efficient and accurate reporting to other bodies.

Indeed, the questionnaire confirmed our general impression from talking to headteachers that centralized school records are used to report, not only to parents, teachers and employers but to a great variety of educational, social and legal agencies. Increasingly, headteachers feel that their existing assessment and reporting systems are inadequate to meet these demands.

In the next section, we shall describe in some detail the procedures whereby the assessment review was set up in Woodvale School. Before that, however, survey results on questions relating to the methods of derivation of school assessment policies are discussed.

How are policies derived?

We asked heads to indicate which of their staff were involved in the formulation of school policies and to describe the methods whereby this was achieved. Not surprisingly, heads and their deputies were most involved but our results also showed that about 45 per cent of heads of department and heads of year and about a third of other teachers were involved in some way when school policies were set up. Various methods of consultation were employed including working parties of senior staff (62 per cent), whole staff meetings (52 per cent) and teacher working parties (47 per cent). Less common were the circulation of discussion papers (32 per cent) and the individual working alone (22 per cent). Obviously some schools used more than one method.

We also asked the head teachers' opinions as to the effectiveness of these various methods of consultation. Many heads favoured small working parties as the most efficient method. As one head put it, 'Small groups, informally, always seem the best way to initiate change, followed by discussion papers and full staff meetings'. Another explained, 'Some individuals were able to present original schemes which would not even have been presented had all discussions been in staff meetings'.

There seemed to be a general recognition of the importance of involving all staff. One head put it like this:

Individual departmental discussions are effective in that all are involved. Young teachers are supported in some cases by more experienced teachers and so helpful discussion and advice takes place with regard to assessment procedures.

We gained the clear impression from the open-ended responses to these questions that the role of the head was absolutely vital in the initial formulation of school policies.

A description in some detail of the development of a school assessment policy at Woodvale School illustrates some of the issues and problems which arise. An LEA in-service course on assessment seems to have provided the initial impetus to action in this school. The head and two senior staff attended this course, which spanned a two year period, the second of which was to be spent on school-based development work on some aspect of assessment.

The school review began with discussions between the management team and, first, heads of department and then teachers within each subject area. These meetings were informal and exploratory. From the beginning, staff were invited to consider precisely what it was they were assessing in their day-to-day classroom practice, and moreover, why they were doing it. Indeed, they were asked to justify the very existence of their subject on the curriculum and this, inevitably, led to a consideration of fundamental questions about the aims and objectives of teaching a particular subject. It also resulted in a temporary retreat from consideration of the question of assessment. To consider assessment first, it was decided, was putting the cart before the horse, and the staff decided on a school-wide curricular review.

For twelve months the curriculum of the school was reviewed through a school-based in-service programme. Teachers met after school, approximately once every three weeks, to discuss ideas and progress. It is important to note that teachers traditionally attend in-service programmes at this school as individuals, rather than as members with different statuses within a department. A probationary Scale 1 teacher is thus given as much of a hearing at these meetings as a departmental head. At the beginning of the course a little under 50 per cent of the staff attended, but attendance rose to over 75 per cent by the end of the year. This, according to the assistant head, was because staff realized that later decisions by the management team would be greatly influenced by what was said at these meetings. During the year's course, using the 11–16 criteria from the HMI Report (GB, DES, 1979) as a basis for discussion, teachers were encouraged to look beyond their own subject, to the whole school curriculum. The head and assistant heads hoped that, by meeting together in this way, teachers would become more aware of the common ground between them, of the opportunities for cross-fertilization of ideas, of sharing resources. The value of such an exercise cannot be easily measured but did any concrete changes occur as a result?

Subject organization shifted from a departmental basis to a faculty structure. There are now six faculties: science, mathematics, language and communication, humanities, design and physical education. Of these, science, mathematics and physical education remain virtually unaffected by the change. The English and modern language departments make up the language and communication faculty, but this remains a loose association; effectively they are still run as separate departments. The biggest changes have come within the new humanities faculty, which includes history, geography, economics, European studies, politics and religious education. Although these subjects are at present taught separately, much ground work has been carried out on integration, and according to the assistant head, the constituent departments are now 'really gelling together'. In the design faculty, the arts and technical departments are attempting a similar exercise.

Apart from this shift to a faculty structure (sealed by the permanent appointment, on scale 4, of chairmen of the six faculties), several other tangible curricular changes resulted from the review. The inclusion of a modern language became compulsory for all pupils in years 1-3 and a new 'common-core' curriculum was designed for this. The number of options pupils may take at the end of the year was reduced from six to five. Together with this change, more time was allocated to English and mathematics. Finally, the timetable organization, which had been based on a forty period week, was changed to a twenty period week; this has not altered the overall balance of subjects on the timetable very much, but allows for fewer disruptive changes in the day.

After one year spent on the curricular review, attention was then focused back again on to problems of assessment. Work has been going on to produce subject assessment profiles, with an initial brief to draw up pilot schemes for the first year (11–12-year-old pupils), though in some cases, they were applicable to other years. Although this was planned to take one term, it took a whole year! Some departments, for example those comprising the humanities faculty, worked at faculty level. Others, such as the English and modern language departments, drew up departmental profiles. The profiles were intended to mirror the efforts of both staff and pupils in working towards the set goals. They were intended to monitor both pupil achievement and teacher effectiveness. Implicit in point (a) of Table 3 is the notion of assessment as the beginning of a diagnostic process, not an end in itself. Staff were encouraged to recognize, in a practical way, the emphasis on the individual pupil, which is so central to the school's philosophy. On the actual construction of profiles, departments were given less direction. The management team was happy for teachers to approach the task in different ways though, ideally, they would have liked profiles to be based on consideration of a subject's underpinning structures or ideas.

Some of the profiles produced are based almost entirely on the content of material to be learnt. For example, the mathematics profile consists of a record of achievement of pre-specified performance levels for the topics covered (fractions, decimals, statistics, etc.) together with a comment on pupils' 'social' attributes. The 'social' part of this profile requires separate assessment of reliability, initiative, motivation, punctuality, sociability, cooperation and presentation on a three-point scale $(++, +, -)$.

The science department by contrast drew up a profile based more on the learning processes characteristic of science (if not unique to it). Thus, teachers are required to assess a pupil's ability to solve problems, to handle data, to manipulate apparatus, etc., as well as more general skills of communication, listening and writing. These are recorded in different ways on the science profile. So, for example, scores of tests are recorded (together with a comment) under sub-headings such as 'problem solving', 'data handling' and 'knowledge of concepts'. It is also noted whether help is needed (none, some, a lot), for example in problem solving/method work, and this record is again supplemented by comments where appropriate. More general skills such as talking and listening and safety skills are assessed periodically by a tick or a cross, together with a comment.

At faculty level, the process of drawing up a profile with at least some elements common to several subjects has proved lengthy. After sixty hours' work (15 meetings), the humanities staff agreed on a very provisional profile. This has taken so long, according to the head of faculty, partly because it was decided to include comment on the general and social development of children. Staff felt that this important area could not be sidestepped, since it constituted an integral part of learning in the humanities. Another problem has been the contentious inclusion of an optional space on the profile for comment by teachers on the success or otherwise of their own performance.

In most of these cases departments have imposed a structured approach to assessment on existing curricula, though, as already mentioned, some minor curricular modifications had been made. Several teachers, wary of the amount of time to be expended, stressed that a key factor in the acceptance of new methods of assessment was the existence of a broad congruence with current practice.

Most of the departmental profiles now require further development and modification. The variety in style of profile is seen as a good thing, but it is anticipated that some departments will need more help and guidance than others on further development work. Some cross-fertilization of ideas across departments may occur at this stage too.

The next task at Woodvale is to decide which information from departmental profiles should be transferred to a centralized school system and what additional information, if any, needs to be included. This work is currently in progress. Our account is therefore not a 'finished story' but describes an on-going development. Comment on it will be deferred until the final section of this chapter.

The approach whereby subject profiles are drawn up within an agreed theoretical framework, and the information then amalgamated to produce a composite school profile, is not the only possible one. However, one head who answered our questionnaire had experienced difficulties with the opposite approach (i.e., working down from the school to the departmental level). He explained, 'The difficulty in applying a whole school policy has resulted in each department being allowed to develop its own method within flexible guidelines'.

Analysis of survey data showed that 55 per cent of heads of departments and year groups felt their own assessment policies were determined in some way by school policy. Of the 100 teachers who gave further explanation of this influence, 36 reported that there was a standardized grading system throughout the school to which they adhered. Typically, as already mentioned, this was a five-point A–E scale, which sometimes included assessment of effort as well as achievement. Indeed, almost all the 'influences' described concerned common grading or examining systems. A few heads of departments and year groups did refer to some general ideological influence from school policy. For example, one explained 'The ethos of the assessment practices at this school (i.e., child-centred) affects "philosophically" the way in which we approach the whole matter'.

Factors affecting the way in which policies are derived

We also asked headteachers to what extent people and factors external to the school had influenced the process of establishing an assessment policy.

The demands of the public examination system would seem, for example, to be far-reaching. Seventy-three per cent of secondary school heads (and even 24 per cent of those from middle schools) said that assessment of 11–14-year-olds was influenced by this. The open-ended responses indicated that, understandably, this was particularly so in 13+ comprehensives. For example, one head explained, 'In a 13–18 school it would seem sensible to have a consistent pattern of assessment for 13–16-year-olds'. However, in other schools too, the early need for selection for option choices was evident, 'In those subjects offered for examination, assessment in the third year (13+) is coloured by the levels of grading at 16+'.

By contrast, there appeared to be very little imposition of LEA assessment requirements on school policies – only ten per cent of heads reported an influence from this source. However, a fifth of our sample had used advice or information provided by LEA advisers.

Not surprisingly, since we were focusing on 11–14-year-olds, there was little influence on policy from local liaison schemes to provide profiles for employers. Only 19 per cent of the secondary schools in our sample were involved in such schemes anyway.

Governors had influenced assessment policy in only six per cent of schools, though a majority of heads had communicated with them on assessment matters either through meetings or through head-teachers' reports.

How are assessment policies organized?

Which aspects of assessment are covered by school policies? Table 4 gives a summary of results on this question. The percentages were similar for middle and secondary schools in all but two of these aspects of assessment, thus indicating a general pattern across school types. Most policies emphasized comparison of individual performances with those of year groups or sets. Two thirds of the middle schools, but only half the secondary schools, included any method of relating the performances of an individual over time and, therefore, of recording progress sequentially. Fifty-eight per cent of middle schools but 88 per cent of secondary schools awarded some grade for effort – a five-point scale was the most common method.

About a quarter of the sample reported that marks were standardized (see Table 4) but open-ended responses indicated that in almost all cases this 'standardization' involved either the use of standardized tests or the crude application of a notional normal distribution curve to assessment results. Further evidence for these interpretations of the word 'standardized' came from responses to a question asking about marks recorded in the centralized school system. Thirty-five per cent of headteachers reported that their school records were standardized but either standardized tests or five-point grading systems were cited. (In drawing up the question, we had in mind some kind of scaling procedure to facilitate inter-subject comparability.)

In nearly half the schools the system included some combination of continuous and periodic assessments. There was evidence of

Table 4: The scope of school assessment policies

Aspects of assessment covered by school policy	% schools (n=97)
A system of record keeping	92%
A system of assessments relating performance of individuals to performance of a whole year group	85%
A system of awarding marks or ratings or grades for effort	76%
A system of assessments relating performances of individuals to performance in their group or set	71%
A system of grading work	64%
A system of assessments relating performances to individuals' own past performances	51%
A system for combining continuous assessments with periodic assessments	49%
A system for standardizing marks in order, for example, to compare performances in different subjects and across different years	26%

Heads of schools without a written policy were asked to respond to the questionnaire in terms of the implicit policies which their current practice reflects. The figures in the table are therefore percentages of all respondents.

departmental variation on this, as one head explained: 'Departments may exercise preference for weighting between work-in-progress and tests, provided the scheme is acceptable'. We did not assume that all these assessments were recorded centrally and asked separately about this. About four out of ten school record-keeping systems contain results of published tests – either attainment or diagnostic. Proportionately twice as many middle schools as secondary recorded results of published tests of attainment. Since few standardized tests are available for subjects other than language and mathematics, this result may reflect a predominant concern with these 'basic' subjects in middle schools. Results of continuous assessments were recorded in just over half the sample and in 60 per cent informal teacher assessments of personal and attitudinal characteristics were noted. Tests of speaking, listening and conversation were each recorded in less than ten per cent of schools and only six schools in the sample included the results of pupil self-assessment in central records.

Our results indicated that, generally, teachers had easy access to central records; if access was not direct it was mediated through senior staff. Parents were allowed access to the school records in only 37 per cent of the sample. The head who replied, 'We believe that parents are entitled to demand/request access to any records we keep on their children', was atypical. Most responses sounded more wary – for example, 'If they ask. No-one has yet done so', and, 'We have never had such a request – it might be difficult to refuse'.

Assessment for transfer

A large majority of schools (82 per cent) reported that their school policy included liaison on assessment with contributing and/or receiving schools. This seemed a most encouraging finding. The open-ended responses on the questionnaire, however, indicated that the figure encompassed a great variety of practice. Some responses, like the ones below, indicated a minimum of inter-school contact. One head reported, 'Some liaison but information given by primary schools is sparse', and another, 'Except in so far as heads meet to consider general aspects – nothing specific'. However, others did suggest a more detailed liaison. One head explained that, 'To some extent our syllabus and assessment of it is a continuous process – from primary through to high. In all subjects liaison with high schools is very good', and another that in her school there was,

'Detailed liaison; teacher meetings; teacher exchange; consensus transfer record produced; detailed mathematics record card from infant school to entry at 11+'.

Our impression from talking to heads, teachers and advisers, however, is that such cooperation is unusual. Suspicion and ignorance of practice in other types of school is common. Specifically, the use of different standardized tests by different primary/ middle schools renders impossible any sensible interpretation of in-coming data by the senior school. Problems associated with transfer have recently been studied in detail in one LEA (Stillman and Maychell, 1984). Our Advisory Group suggested that this was an area of considerable interest and that it was a particularly acute problem for 13+ schools.

It was for this reason that we visited Highfield School (a 13+ high school with 1,300 pupils), the top tier of a pyramid of fifteen schools which gives unusual priority to liaison and coordination of effort. The aim of this special study was to describe how coordination is effected between schools in the pyramid (one high school, six middle schools and eight first schools) with particular reference to assessment procedures, and to identify, if possible, some criteria of good practice. To this end we held informal interviews with the head and senior staff of the high school (four heads of department and head of lower year) and with the heads of three middle schools and one first school. The following description and comment is based on the field notes made at these interviews.

Coordination, in the opinion of the head of the high school, must begin with a coordinated view of the needs of the area. Schools at all levels are thus seen as 'links in a chain of permanent education', with foundations laid at the ages of five, seven, thirteen and at sixteen years old having equal value and relevance. Work on achieving these aims had a modest beginning more than ten years ago with inter-school meetings which resulted first in some discussions on matters such as school hours, holidays, lunch arrangements and welfare services. Heads began to consider the pyramid as an entity, to meet regularly (several times a term) and they have done so since then.

The schools put much effort into easing the general process of transfer at 13+. The head of the high school takes a 'travelling circus' separately to all the middle schools. At these informal meetings parents of the transferees hear about the high school organization and curriculum from a 'panel' of people, including the head, two deputy heads, the head of year, the school counsellor and two student tutors (fifth form pupils who have finished their examinations). Student tutors also spend some time helping the younger pupils when they visit the high school.

The high school places its new entrants into four bands. Allocation to these is based on a rank order of pupils from the six middle schools. The compilation of rank orders is left to the individual middle school – all use the same tests (some standardized and some teacher-written) but teacher opinion also influences the order. Comparable assessment records are passed on for language work, mathematics and French from all the middle schools. There seems to be a general recognition that the middle school class teachers know their pupils well and that the responsibility for ranking should therefore be theirs. However, the ultimate decision about which band a pupil goes into lies with the head of year and appropriate colleagues in the high school. The social development of pupils is discussed in detail and the formation of tutor groups involves much liaison between middle school teachers and pastoral care staff at the high school. At the curricular level, the degree of cooperation so far achieved varies from one subject area to another.

The same 'common-core' syllabus for mathematics is taught in the final two years of the middle schools and an assessment of this (consisting of two test papers) ensures that the high school receives a set of comparable scores. Common tests provide information on reading ages at 7,9,11 and 13 years and, in addition, all pupils take part of the Richmond Test battery prior to transfer, so the high school receives comparable scores in the field of language as well. In French there is a three year foundation course – two years in the middle schools and one in the high school. A common assessment in French is made at the end of the final middle school year. This consists of tests of listening comprehension, reading comprehension, oracy and written composition. The written component is seen by the high school to be the most discriminating for setting purposes. In science a core syllabus for the final middle school year was drawn up – this includes broad topics such as heat and reproduction but avoids an excessively prescriptive specification of content. There are no common assessment procedures as yet in science. Curricular coordination has recently been extended to a number of other subject areas – to remedial education, the humanities and music. Similar efforts in the areas of religious education and social and moral education are planned.

Bald statements detailing agreements about syllabuses and assessment procedures give little indication of the hard collaborative work that went into their achievement. In some cases middle schools have lost a little autonomy in decision-making about curricular content and assessment, but all the heads we interviewed stressed that the advantages to their children more than compensated for this loss.

Several factors, which could be interpreted as criteria for good practice, emerged as reasons for the success of coordination so far achieved in this pyramid.

Although the head of the high school argues that a pyramid structure is not necessary to achieve coordination, this pyramid is of manageable size. It is not scattered geographically but is self-contained, with almost all pupils in the area going to one high school. In this respect, the situation compares favourably with the not unusual arrangement of a high school receiving pupils from thirty or forty schools.

Secondly, heads stressed that pyramid coordination had not been imposed either by central government or by the LEA; rather it evolved gradually from the felt needs of heads and teachers in the schools. Once heads began to discuss the total educational development of children the need for some standardization of procedures for transfer at 9+ and 13+ was recognized.

Heads recognize that to give such priority to pyramid coordination involves a large commitment of time and effort. An obvious factor in its success is their belief that the educational advantages to their pupils merit such effort.

The middle and first schools heads all commented on the positive and non-judgmental attitude of high school staff, and particularly of the head. As one of them put it, '(the head of the high school) walks a tightrope between encroaching on the rights of the feeder schools and satisfying the demands of her staff'. Another head commented, 'You never get the feeling that you're being dictated to – nor that we are feeder streams to the main river'.

Although heads in this pyramid look beyond their own four walls and out to the total educational development of the child, the traditional discrepancy in approach to pedagogy between the primary and secondary sectors remains. One middle school head explained, for example, that he believed firmly in the pedagogic importance of exploratory talk (that is learning through talking) but this belief was not shared by many high school staff. The head of the high school admits that 'the high school specialist can often see the students he receives as tabula rasa on which he intends to scribe his own specialism'. One head described the lack of liaison at staff level, as opposed to head teacher level, to be the pyramid's greatest weakness, and suggested that meaningful liaison should include discussion about pedagogic beliefs and general approaches, as well as more specific discussion of curricular content. In this way, it was thought, some of the very real problems emanating from the different pedagogical perspectives of middle and high school teachers could be tackled. Several interviewees proposed that, ideally, teachers should work for a limited period in the other school to find out at first hand about its day-to-day activities.

This study suggests that, to be effective, liaison between schools has to operate at departmental as well as headteacher level. Coordination of assessment procedures obviously affords pupils some advantage – the comparability of test results for all children makes the whole system fairer, continuity of course work (at least in some subjects) across schools must ease transition. The considerable change in learning approaches which some children experience on transfer is softened. The more general advantages to teachers of frequent, informal inter-school contact are not easy to measure, but several heads and teachers in this pyramid indicated clearly how invaluable they found it.

Dissemination and review of school policies

Once school policies are devised, how are they disseminated throughout the school? Are they reviewed from time to time? Are teachers new to the school informed? We asked headteachers about the implementation of school policy and the coordination of assessment activities within their schools. From the questionnaire results, the most common method of communication with teaching staff was through regular after-school meetings (75 per cent). Only just over a quarter of the sample held review meetings during school hours. Fifty-seven per cent of headteachers reported that they arranged meetings with new members of staff to discuss policy and practice. Written schemes were issued to all members of staff in 42 per cent of the schools in the sample.

Thirty-nine per cent of schools had a member of staff who was designated as coordinator of assessment and most of these were responsible for coordinating practices between departments or year groups. Not surprisingly, more secondary schools (47 per cent) had such posts than middle schools (26 per cent). Typically, they were deputy or assistant heads, heads of year or other comparable senior posts. Several teachers responded by indicating that their posts had been created recently. Results from the head of department questionnaire agreed well, with 39 per cent of these teachers working in a school with a coordinator for assessment. Heads of departments or years reported a variety of help and guidance given by these post-holders ranging from simple administrative instruction to guidelines for grading, advice about the applicability of various tests and use of statistical procedures.

Two thirds of headteachers stated that formal means of review of assessment policy existed in their schools. Typically, these reviews took place at meetings either of whole staffs, or smaller groups (departments, year groups, etc).

Sorting out the issues and the problems

The research results reported in this chapter raise some important questions and obviously many schools have only just begun to consider these issues.

Is assessment an activity marginal to educational purposes or is it an integral and indispensable part of teaching and learning? The general attitude to this question in the school seems to us to be determined to a large extent by the headteacher. The head who wrote:

> Much work still has to be done in encouraging staff to look at patterns of assessment. I find that teachers are reluctant to formalize an activity which they are engaged in daily,

makes a strong point. Teachers, he implies, do not associate 'assessment' with day-to-day classroom evaluation. It seems to be the formalization of assessment policies and procedures which worries some, like the head who explained:

> My own commitment is to helping teachers become sensitive observers of the behaviours of children. Written assessments are literally not worth the paper on which they are written.

It may be however, that observational assessment of children's classroom activities, if discussed and structured, could provide more reliable assessments for these particular aims.

In any case, the general tenor of replies to a question about desired improvements indicated that most heads see the need for coordination and acknowledge that this probably involves some written statement of policy.

If this policy is to be more than a set of prescribed procedures it will specify the purposes of assessment within the school. The policy will include, at least implicitly, not only the 'how', but the 'why'. It seems likely that many who object to formalization of assessment throughout the school would be happier with this approach. At Woodvale School, for example, the process began with some fundamental thinking about ideals and objectives and an assessment policy is developing which meets the needs of this particular school; it is neither 'imposed' nor 'tagged on', but is perceived as necessary and integral. The curricular question, 'Are we doing what we say we are trying to do in the best possible ways?' can only be answered, however, partially and tentatively, by some assessment of learning and teaching. It must logically be followed by the assessment question, 'How do we know how much pupils have learned, how well we have taught?'

Apart from advantages of some rationalization of procedures there are some issues which must, we think, be decided as a matter of school policy. One very important one is the question of assessment of personal attributes. At Woodvale School, anxiety was expressed about the ethics of including personal attributes (of motivation, honesty, social skills, etc.) on assessment profiles. This is a thorny issue and one we encountered many times. On the one hand, such factors are the justifiable concern of educators and, indeed, an integral part of learning – to ignore them is to take a narrow view of the purposes of education. On the other hand, assessment (and recording) of such factors is thought to be extremely difficult; indeed, it is even open to abuse.

But we would not want to over-emphasize the importance of written policy statements. At Woodvale, senior staff stressed that documentation including theoretical guidelines, profiles, etc. was a minor end product. The processes of teachers thinking, discussing (and occasionally arguing!) about what they are doing and why they are doing it, formed by far the most valuable outcome. The mechanisms of decision-making have changed in that school. It has become more consultative generally, with increased involvement of junior teachers. The necessity of fostering a good climate was emphasised – this involved getting the cooperation of the staff from the beginning, not imposing rigid time-scales (and, particularly, not pushing the pace of change), and not having too firm, preconceived ideas about the means of achieving goals which were, nevertheless, clearly specified. The order of activities did not proceed according to plan but remained flexible; the curricular review was, in a sense, a tangent, yet it was an absolutely necessary response to a perceived need by the teachers. At Lambourne School, where the common grading system had been introduced throughout the school, the deputy head responsible for its introduction was obliged to adopt a consultative approach (because the exercise was being monitored for higher degree work at a local Polytechnic, it had been decided to interview teachers beforehand about their practices and opinions). This, he said frankly, had been against his better judgment. However, he later admitted that these interviews and consultations had contributed crucially to the acceptance of the scheme. Such a view was expressed repeatedly in our questionnaire replies. There was much evidence that the schools which had adopted consultative procedures had found the results worthwhile, if very time-consuming. One head put it like this, 'The working parties and department meetings have given a sense of purpose and involvement. Progress is inevitably slow because of entrenched attitudes'.

It is clear that LEAs are right to support schools in their own efforts to improve assessment practice, and not to impose. The headteachers at both Woodvale and Highfield schools made the point that initiatives came from the school, not from the LEA, although in both cases the advisory service had been very influential.

What are the constraints for schools on making improvements in assessment policies? Our questionnaire results indicated that time was, predictably, the main one (36 per cent of our sample said that time was a major constraint). Consultative procedures of review to formulate an agreed policy are time-consuming in themselves. The management team at Woodvale was well aware of this. As the assistant head put it 'we are in debt before we start', the review must be 'cost-effective' and teachers must feel that something useful (perhaps ultimately time-saving) will come out of it. Teachers are interested in assessment, but if they are to change their practice, the new system must be simple and quick and its value must be clear. A head reiterated these same concerns on the questionnaire when he cited a major problem as, 'Producing convincing arguments for change and including the changes in an acceptable minimum time-scale for effective completion by teachers'.

The questionnaire returns suggest that heads are also concerned about the lack of teacher expertise on assessment. One head, when asked about constraints, explained:

Time – the time required by staff to complete profiles – would be additional work to their day, not substituting or replacing teaching time.

Knowledge – teachers lack knowledge of how to assess, methods to use, lack judgment of value of many standardized tests which are available. All are not aware that they lack the knowledge.

In conclusion, it would seem that the existence of written statements of school policy on assessment results in some rationalization of procedures. Ideally, such policies should incorporate a recognition of the integral part assessment plays in the teaching and learning processes within the school and a consideration of the various purposes to which assessments are put. The question of a school's responsibility with regard to assessment of pupils' personal attributes remains contentious and difficult. Finally, it seems that consultative procedures – though frequently time-consuming and somewhat unpredictable – constitute the best method for achieving workable schemes. Teachers' justifiable doubts about disproportionately large amounts of time being spent on assessment must be recognized and respected. There is some evidence though, that once teachers become convinced of the value of assessment as a useful educational exercise, these doubts are at least partly allayed.

Chapter 3

Assessment at Departmental Level

Problems of definition

This chapter reports findings from the questionnaire survey of holders of 'middle management' posts in schools. Schools of course use different names for such posts; secondary schools typically have heads of department and/or year, whilst middle schools have staff who may be specialists and coordinate subject areas or year groups but who usually teach the whole curriculum. One hundred and eighty teachers from secondary schools and forty-three from middle schools responded. We addressed this questionnaire to heads of department, heads of year groups and holders of posts of special responsibility – it was designed to be answered by those teachers who coordinated or were responsible for some specified area of school activities, whether in a paid capacity or not. For the sake of brevity we refer to this level of the survey as the 'departmental' level, but the reader is asked to bear in mind the heterogeneous nature of this group of respondents when considering the results reviewed below.

In addition to the survey results two special studies which exemplify aspects of good practice are referred to in this chapter. They are:

An LEA scheme of graded objectives and tests in modern languages.

A departmental scheme for assessment linked to public examination requirements in an 11+ comprehensive (Arndale School).

Policies and practices

The problem of distinguishing between policies and practices exists at this level as well as at school level. We decided to regard statements about both procedures and intentions (or purposes) of assessment as policies and assumed that these could be in the form of either a written document or a verbal agreement. In fact, there were far fewer written documents at this level than at that of the school. A much greater proportion of heads of department, however, claimed that agreed aims and procedures had been established. Eighty-eight per cent of respondents reported that an agreed set of teaching aims existed, and 83 per cent that all department members accepted a set of assessment procedures. However, these procedures were written down in less than a third of departments.

Only 28 per cent of departments had formalized their policies to the extent of producing a document. For communication of departmental policy to new members of staff, most departmental heads relied on discussion and explanation and on departmental meetings. A few said they had formal induction procedures, while others worked through a moderation exercise with new staff to attempt to bring marking within departmental guidelines.

The relationship between departmental policies and school policies was explored and in 55 per cent of cases it was reported that school policy did have some effect on departmental practice. Some departments used the school grading system and were required by school policy to set a common examination for all pupils within a year group. The translation of marks and grades into a distribution which was explicitly stated to be 'balanced' was less prevalent. None of the school assessment policies that included balancing procedures took account of possible year-to-year variations or differences between sets in a year (as mentioned briefly in Chapter 2). Most schemes divided their student groups into five levels, with instructions that a fixed proportion be placed in each level. So, for example, level one might contain 10 per cent of the group, level two 20 per cent, level three 40 per cent, level four 20 per cent and level five 10 per cent – in a set of thirty pupils, three would then always receive grade A, six grade B, twelve grade C, six grade D and three grade E. This procedure appears to make grades comparable across subjects and classes but it can obscure important differences when attainment in different sets varies. The distribution described above imposes a common pattern across teaching sets, whereas in fact there is unlikely to be a general norm. Some schools reported using percentage marks allocated to give a 'normal' distribution; but again it is invalid to assume that attainment in a year or set will be distributed normally. Only by some form of scaling can marks from different subjects be compared. Since school and departmental policies do often require comparison of assessments we consider a hypothetical example in Figure 1 below.

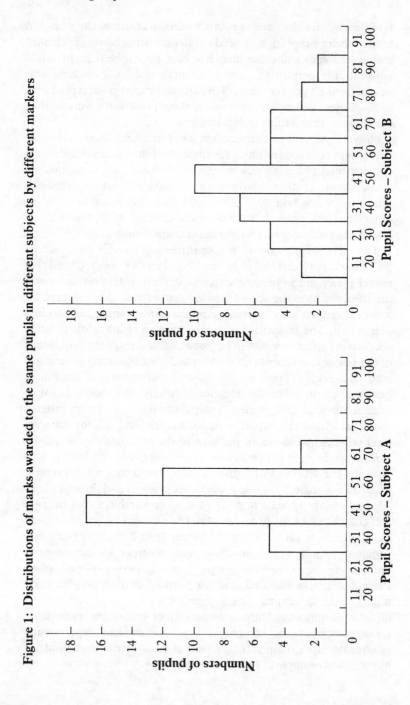

Figure 1: Distributions of marks awarded to the same pupils in different subjects by different markers

Figure 1 shows the distribution of marks awarded to a set of pupils in two subjects, by different markers. It can be seen at a glance that the set has attracted a very different pattern of marks for the two subjects. Variations like this could be caused by a differential pattern of attainment across subjects, or by differences in individual teachers' marking styles. In certain circumstances scores from two or more subjects are added together; in others scores from different teachers of the same subject are combined. In both types of combination problems can occur. If the scores are simply added, the set of scores which is more widely dispersed (in Figure 1, this is subject B) has a greater effect on the final distribution of pupils, as determined by their marks. There would be a likelihood of more tied marks in subject A than in B. Subject B extends the top and bottom of the scale and would tend to hold pupils in these relative positions, against the influence of subject A scores.

Inconsistencies of this kind have led some schools to introduce scaling procedures. One school we visited has computerized the data handling, which has greatly eased teacher work-loads; another uses score conversion graphs. Scaling marks leaves pupils in the same order of attainment but allows scores to be compared across subjects because their dispersions are equated. Such procedures are useful when, for example, a group of children is taught a subject by more than one teacher or when pupils are regrouped (say when forming an examination set from the tops of several classes). In these cases, whenever possible, common assessments should be used and marks should be scaled. Further examples and some issues arising from the comparison and combination of assessment results are explored more fully in Chapter 5.

Scope of departmental policies

Most policies specified both the methods of assessment and the system of awarding and collating marks or grades. Seventy-two per cent of heads of department gave guidance to department members about assessment methods. A summary of responses to a question asking about the main methods employed is given in Table 5 and illustrates a rich variety of procedures in operation in our sample of schools. The list ranges over continuous assessment, standardized (published) tests, mental arithmetic tests, worksheet assessments, pupil self-assessment, grades for topics, impression grades, etc.

Schemes commonly included two or three methods, chosen to reflect the mix of content and teaching approaches within the department or sector of responsibility. In all, more than forty styles of assessment were reported, evidence which suggests an encouraging variety of approach. Seventy per cent of departments specifed the mark or grade system to be used and 61 per cent of departmental heads took responsibility for collecting and collating assessments made by their staff members.

Table 5: Main methods of departmental assessments which are recorded

Data sheet for Q.12 heads of department questionnaire (Appendix I) with methods listed, together with frequencies of mention.

Written examinations 138	Objective tests following each module 2
Practicals 53	
Objective tests 50	Pupil self-assessment 2
Tests 18	Oral/aural 2
Written tests 17	Own design graded tests 2
Continuous assessment 17	Essays 1
Oral 16	Tests of physical skill 1
Homework 15	Assessment of effort and attitude 1
Character/personality summary 13	Mental arithmetic tests 1
Exams including objectively marked and free writing sections 12	Common exam for all feeder schools 1
	Impression grades 1
Classwork teacher assessments 12	Subjective assessment of physical skills 1
Section tests 9	Observation 1
Short teacher tests 6	'O' level style objective tests 1
Homework and classwork 6	Games ability 1
Grades for topics 5	A general grade 1
Effort marks 5	Course work 1
Standardized tests for screening 4	Exercises 1
Written work 4	Group discussion 1
Classwork 3	Swimming ability 1
Initial objective tests 3	Projects 1
Writing up notes 3	Points test 1
Regular written work 3	Oral and classwork 1
Essay tests 3	Continuous assessment practicals 1

Survey results also indicated that a large proportion of heads of department are aware of the need for continual review; some 60 per cent of them made a periodic review of practices as a matter of policy.

Forty-two per cent of the departments surveyed also said they would aim to use their assessments as a basis for a reappraisal of teaching. Mathematics and remedial departments were more likely to relate assessment results to teaching and the curriculum generally than English, humanities and modern languages departments.

Only 30 per cent of departments helped teachers to find effective ways of using assessment results for feedback to pupils. Two thirds of English and remedial departments expected teachers to use assessments in this way, but generally departmental heads did not emphasize this aspect of assessment; it seems that impact on the pupil is not usually a major consideration. In only a very few schools are pupils actually given an opportunity to assess themselves.

Derivation and coordination of departmental policies

Derivation

Headteachers and heads of department have the authority to formulate assessment policies entirely alone. However, this approach appears to be unusual. Both headteachers (working at the level of the school) and heads of department commonly set up consultative procedures. When comparison was made between departments with assessment policies and those without, it was quite clear that most of the departments with developed policies had used consultation. Moreover, these heads of department recognized the value of such an approach.

In our sample, 71 per cent of heads of department had been instrumental in drawing up their own department's policies and 50 per cent had involved department members. Some policies would of course have been inherited. When consultation is effective it is likely that the details of departmental procedures have been negotiated rather than merely presented for approval. Consultation implies more than this, however, since policies need to be communicated to and be understood by everyone concerned.

It was evident from our survey that few teachers, including heads of departments, are equipped to pursue the technical problems which may arise when setting up or reviewing assessment policies. We visited a number of schools where teachers had been involved in a year-long LEA course on assessment. These teachers had provided invaluable support to other staff during their school's reviewing procedures. Assessment would seem to be a most fruitful area for LEA in-service provision.

Coordination

It is one thing to have a policy, but another to ensure that it is implemented consistently. In our sample, 39 per cent of schools had coordinators for assessment; in many of them coordination was part of the headteacher's responsibility, but in others a senior member of staff took the role. A comparison of headteachers' and heads' of department replies showed that 27 per cent of those schools with coordinators had no written policy document, whereas 63 per cent of those with a written policy document also had a coordinator for assessment. The most common functions performed by the cordinator were translation of departmental marks into the school-wide grading system and organization of meetings to discuss and formulate policy and procedures. Coordinators were more common in secondary schools in the sample, especially those with an age range of 11–16 or 11–18 years.

Forty per cent of the respondents reported inter-departmental links on curriculum matters. For example, they reached agreements on the allocation of certain topics or on the order of presentation of ideas and experiences. However, there was little evidence of parallel agreements on assessment procedures; only ten per cent of the departments with curricular links had negotiated a coordinated approach on assessment.

Methods and uses of assessment

Which assessments are recorded?

We asked heads of department to list the main methods of assessment for which results were recorded at departmental level. The vast majority of these were test results; 62 per cent cited written examinations, and objective test results were also often recorded. Other methods were recorded much less often – homework marks or grades, continuous assessment based on periodic tests and assessments of oral work were mentioned far less often.

Eighty-two per cent of departments awarded and recorded marks for effort or application. Typically, these were not based on a regularly-kept record but made impressionistically, once or twice a year, for reporting purposes.

Uses of assessment records

To what use are these departmentally-recorded assessments put? Survey results showed that some 67 per cent of heads of department collect individual teachers' assessments and 77 per cent of these (i.e., 51 per cent of the sample) collate them into a single record. Table 6 shows the uses to which such records are put. Heads of department reported on their use by themselves and by their staffs. The figures given in Table 6 are percentages of respondents who use these methods with most (80-100 per cent) of their pupils.

Table 6: Uses of assessment records by heads of department and their staff (n=149)

Uses of assessment records	Head of department		Teachers in departments	
	Middle school	Secondary school	Middle school	Secondary school
Allocation of pupils to sets or groups	47%	34%	42%	39%
Deciding how to help individual pupils	13%	35%	45%	34%
Reviewing pupil progress overall as a means of assessing the effectiveness of departmental teaching	26%	21%	39%	24%
Reviewing departmental schemes of work	18%	19%	21%	25%
Giving pupils a clear indication of their progress in a year group	50%	40%	39%	49%

It indicates that about 40 per cent of recorded assessments are used to place pupils in sets or groups and rather more (about 45 per cent) to give pupils an indication of their progress. Use of records for review of departmental work schemes was much lower (about 20 per cent). Some of the differences between secondary and middle schools are interesting. For example, in middle schools it seems to be teachers' records which are used to help individual pupils, whereas in secondary schools, heads of department use their collated records for this purpose as much as the teachers in their departments. The figures indicate that middle school teachers make more use of records when looking at the effectiveness of their teaching.

Statistical treatment of assessment results

The survey indicated that very few departments use any form of statistical treatment of results in order to compare results between markers, years or departments. Averages were calculated for departmental marks in 25 per cent of cases and standard deviations in 13 per cent. More sophisticated treatments, such as comparing means on two or more sets of results (13 per cent) and analysis of individual questions in terms of their degree of difficulty (23 per cent), were similarly not common. Only five per cent of departments used computers for processing their assessment results. The most popular statistical treatments were the production of graphs of distribution (29 per cent), classification of pupils in score bands (31 per cent), and transformations of raw scores to another scale (27 per cent). Since many teachers have probably had no training in assessment techniques these figures are perhaps encouraging. They reflect the efforts teachers and in-service course providers have made towards improving standards of practice in schools.

However, it remains generally true that teachers lack knowledge about available methods for ensuring fairer comparisons of pupils and that there is little use of records of pupil performance over time. These findings are perhaps not surprising in view of the low level of in-service training in assessment received by heads of department. Only 23 per cent of our sample had attended such courses and, of these, moderation meetings for examination boards were mentioned most often.

Formal assessments

SCHOOL EXAMINATIONS

Sixty per cent of departments surveyed set a common examination for all 11–12-year-old pupils within a year group; for 13–14-year-old pupils the figure was 67 per cent. Most usually this assessment was made once a year, but some departments examined two, three or more times. Other departments did set separate examinations for pupils of different attainment levels (21 per cent wrote different papers for all sets of 11-year-old pupils and 24 per cent for 14-year-olds). It would seem then that much formal assessment conforms to the conventional picture of school examinations set at widely spaced intervals. Often a single assessment instrument is applied across the whole spectrum of attainment.

Some examinations were devised by individual teachers for sets they themselves teach but more usually examinations contain contributions from both heads of department and teachers. Overall responsibility for setting an examination is often allocated to department members in turn and they collate suggestions from the other staff. Such collaborative efforts are common and sometimes even occur between schools. One middle school in our sample worked with neighbouring schools to construct a common examination for pupil transfer to secondary school.

Similarly, mark-schemes for examinations are typically devised by departments; only 15 per cent reported individual teachers choosing their own schemes. Nearly a third of the heads of department reported a requirement to conform to school policy on grading in some way. In some cases translation to a school-wide system followed marking to a departmental scheme and in others teachers were required to mark initially using the school system. Our findings generally indicated, though, that assessment systems are very much in the hands of departments.

INFLUENCE OF PUBLIC EXAMINATIONS

The survey results also indicated, however, that assessment methods used in public examinations had a considerable influence at departmental level. Forty-seven per cent of departments used methods which conform with those used in public examinations for some or all of the time. Table 7 shows the groups of pupils to which they were applied. It is clear from the table that this influence becomes more pronounced the older the pupils and also the higher their attainment level.

Table 7: Assessments conforming to those used in public examinations

Band or set	Percentage of departments using public examination methods (n=123)		
	for 11–12-year-olds	for 12–13-year-olds	for 13–14-year-olds
High sets or bands	18%	28%	82%
Middle sets or bands	18%	25%	73%
Low sets or bands	11%	15%	54%
Remedial sets or bands	5%	7%	28%

Although predictions about eventual external examination performance were common at 13 years, and were used for allocation to sets or bands, there was little evidence that these predictions were matched against actual public examination results. Only four per cent of departments operated any such internal check on this use of the assessment records of 13–14-year-old pupils. It was more common (23 per cent of cases) for internal records of 14–16-year-old pupils to be correlated with eventual external examination results.

PUBLISHED STANDARDIZED TESTS

A quarter of the departments surveyed used published standardized tests, the major users being heads of year and deputies (26 per cent), remedial departments (24 per cent) and mathematics departments (9 per cent). Since standardized tests of attainment deal mainly with language and mathematics, the overall proportion of departments which use these tests seems high. Thirty different tests were mentioned – the most commonly used being Daniels and Diack, Holborn Reading Scale, Schonell, Neale Analysis (all reading tests), NFER Basic Mathematics tests and unnamed tests of verbal reasoning. Some of the tests mentioned are out of date whilst others produce misleading information, e.g., test content which does not represent a school's curriculum, tables of norms based on inadequate samples and extended to inappropriate ages, reading age scales which are uninterpretable in terms of a child's competence.

Informal assessments

Assessment by tests and examinations is only part of the evaluation of pupils. Teachers assess informally much of the time and we asked heads of department to list the main methods used for such assessment. The evidence suggested an almost complete reliance on written work. Three aspects of pupil performance other than this were assessed – practical work, oracy and listening skills. These, however, were not very common. Assessments of oral work (comprising only five per cent of informal assessments) were used mainly by modern language teachers, although they were also reported by English, science, art, craft and humanities departments. Informal assessments of practical work were associated with aesthetics and craft, physical education and science, but again only a few departments in total reported using them (3 per cent). Listening exercises were even less common and were mentioned by only two per cent of departments.

One small secondary school in the sample made termly checks on teachers' routine impressions of pupil attainment. For this teachers recorded, quickly and without referring to mark books, whether a pupil's progress was satisfactory or unsatisfactory or whether they were undecided. The deputy head of the school monitored these and checked them against other assessment records. He gave particular attention to those pupils about whose progress a teacher was unsure and discussed the classroom experiences of these children to check that they were getting enough teacher attention etc. This system seemed to provide valuable feedback to the teacher on the accuracy of his day-to-day assessments.

Few assessments which are made informally are recorded which is perhaps surprising since many teachers, particularly those in middle schools, have great faith in their validity and their value.

Does assessment change practice?

The primary purpose of assessment in schools is to obtain information about the performance of pupils, but assessment results can also provide valuable feedback on curricular content and on teaching methods. We asked heads of department to describe any such curricular changes that had occurred as a result of examining the pattern of their assessment results. The replies fell broadly into two categories. There were changes in methods of teaching, examining, or content of courses, and changes in grouping and regrouping pupils. One head of history reported that scrutiny of assessment results had led to, 'Introduction of new courses for 14+ based on 11–14 assessment, setting changes within band groups and syllabus changes'. A head of geography explained that a variety of changes had occurred in his department:

> Reorganization of second year pupils into sets, change in curricular content and in modes of assessment. In addition, one person in the department has been made responsible for compiling formal assessments prior to presentation to H.O.D.

Further questions invited heads of department to make suggestions for improvement of existing schemes. Interestingly, the heavy reliance upon examinations did not seem to be based on any great faith in these methods, but on a lack of optimism about staff acceptance of change. Many responses indicated that staff resistance to change was, in their opinion, a major problem. However, many of these heads of department also felt that detailed discussions with department members would be the most fruitful way of overcoming this resistance and working towards change. The majority of respondents saw the instigation of change as the responsibility of the headteacher and senior staff, but a few heads of department mentioned the need for help from outside – for example, from in-service courses and from the advisory service. One head of department explained that, 'Ideally one would like to involve individuals with expertise in assessment and evaluation within the school context and within the authority, but there is no precedent for such liaisons'.

It would seem then, that the need to extend the range of assessment methods is acknowledged. There is also a recognition of the value of consultation, so that all department members can take part in decisions about changes in policy and practice.

Externally-influenced change

Teachers in charge of subject areas do, of course, respond to influences on assessment which are wider in scope than that of the school. Two examples of such externally-influenced change are given below – the first is a description of participation in an LEA graded objectives scheme in French and German, the other describes the response of a school biology department to the requirements of public examinations.

A graded objectives scheme in modern languages

INTRODUCTION

Modern language teachers in certain areas of the country have recently developed schemes of assessment based on graded objectives and the movement appears to be spreading to mathematics and science. The approach illustrates well how assessment can be linked with the curriculum and throws light on the factors which facilitate success in innovation. The aim is to develop good communication skills in a foreign language and to test various levels of performance in the everyday uses of that language. Traditionally, of course, speaking and listening were given very much less attention than writing in modern language teaching.

The graded objectives approach echoes the ideas of mastery learning in which the pupil's performance is compared to the mastery of a task, not to the performance of others. Basically, a syllabus expressed as graded objectives sets out stages in the development of language competencies which are to be taught sequentially. Most children can master the early stages of such schemes and clearly stated criteria of performance are designed to give children a good understanding of their own position relative to these criteria. Pupils are tested at the end of each stage and those passing are given a certificate to indicate this accomplishment. They may then proceed to the next stage. Schemes in modern languages have remained localized, with each authority devising its own, although examination boards are now developing similar schemes.

THE SCHEME

We studied a programme of graded objectives in modern languages operating in one local authority and comment here on the main implications of such schemes for schools. The approach is becoming well known to modern language teachers and so this account is intended mainly for teachers in other disciplines who may find the general approach interesting and applicable to them.

We talked with teachers at eight schools, both middle and secondary, and had interviews with the adviser for modern languages and the head of the LEA language teaching development centre. In this authority, development has remained very much in the hands of the teachers, with LEA funding and support channelled through the advisory service. The language teaching information centre (itself part of the advisory service) organizes working parties of teachers and administers the scheme. Two graded levels were developed at first but there are now separate working parties for three levels. Tests at all levels have three sections which assess listening comprehension, reading comprehension and speaking.

THE PHILOSOPHY

Behind the general intended outcome of development of competence lie two basic principles. One is that provision of a programme which contains short-term, realizable objectives is motivating for pupils. The other is that using real-life simulations is a more natural and meaningful way to learn another language. This method is perhaps particularly suited to those pupils who will do no further academic study of the language. The implications of these principles are well rehearsed in the literature (e.g., Buckby, 1980; Harding, Page and Rowell, 1980; Harrison, 1982). Oral testing procedures follow from the use of a teaching method that uses real-life situations and role play. Few of the teachers we interviewed adopted this 'pure' version of the graded objectives approach; most mixed in traditional grammar-based lessons. Working parties in this authority believe strongly in constructing new test papers every year. This process takes up a great deal of time – fortnightly meetings over a half-yearly period.

In the early years of the scheme, tests for levels one and two were administered only towards the end of a school year. It has now been decided that previous tests will be made available during the year for pupils to take as they become ready. This will improve the scheme but not reduce the amount of work required of teachers, since new questions and assessment schemes are still written each year.

WORKING PARTIES

It is clear that the working parties have been an excellent source of in-service training for their teacher members, the experience of the long-serving members being passed on to newly-involved teachers. Teachers told us that most discussion centred on the acceptability of certain usage, on the difficulties of distinguishing between 'communicative competence' and traditional grammar-based ideas of competence, and on the standards appropriate to each level. This latter point remains particularly problematic. Middle school teachers viewed the scheme as appropriate for pupils of all abilities and pupils who were capable of progressing through all three levels did so. Other pupils, of course, made slower progress and never attained the third level. However, some of the secondary schools used graded objective tests as an alternative to CSE for lower attaining groups. Teachers using graded tests for this purpose tended to disapprove of the high pass rate and of the difficulty of level three. Their objections are really, however, based on a misunderstanding of the purposes of the scheme. It was clear from our discussions that such misunderstandings were even more likely to arise with teachers who had not participated in working parties and who thus had no direct involvement. Some of these teachers reported that guidance notes for the syllabus had been insufficient to gauge the required standards for each level.

An important problem with teacher-controlled curriculum groups is that, being voluntary, their continued existence is not ensured. In this case, however, the groups have been able to recruit new members as old ones leave. Turnover is relatively slow, with most teachers serving for well over a year, despite the large commitment of time and energy.

SOME CONCLUDING REMARKS ON THE SCHEME

The teachers interviewed were in general agreement about the advantages and disadvantages of this local authority initiative.

The main advantage of the scheme is undoubtedly that this method of teaching and assessment seems to motivate pupils of all abilities, a factor particularly important for middle schools with their mixed ability groupings. Several reservations were also expressed. The tests are sometimes used as end-of-term, or more usually end-of-year tests; a procedure which entirely contravenes the intention behind graded objectives. It is organizationally difficult and time-consuming to test a child as and when he becomes ready to move to a higher level and for this reason most teachers resorted to testing all their pupils at one time. A second misuse of the scheme which worried some of the working party teachers was that tests of graded objectives could be tacked on to a pre-existing course with little change in teaching method. This tended to occur in departments where there had been little or no contact with the teacher groups. It seems clear that headteachers and heads of department need to be alerted to these possible misuses, particularly if graded tests in this and other areas of the curriculum are to be applied more widely.

Although this assessment scheme is organized at the level of the local authority, it is basically 'teacher controlled'. Any nationally-agreed, graded curricula and tests will present schools with a choice between internal and external schemes. Arguments for the latter will focus on standards and on accountability, although pupils' progress and efforts may be better evaluated from within the school. National public examinations do, of course, constitute a strong external influence on school assessment procedures, yet teachers have relatively little control over them. Of course, the response to external assessment requirements can be far more positive than merely adopting grading structures or rehearsing examination questions.

One department's response to public examination requirements

We visited the biology department of an 11+ comprehensive, Arndale School, where requirements of public examinations heavily influence approaches to teaching. The special study reported below describes the development of a biology course for third year pupils, a curricular innovation which arose, not from modifications of a published scheme, but from the needs perceived within one department.

The teacher who designed the course, into which assessment instruments were incorporated to monitor pupil progress throughout the year, acknowledges that the approach to teaching reflects the requisites of public examinations. An analysis of the skills required for 'O' level and CSE biology examinations provided the foundation for the new course design. Such an orientation would not, of course, appeal to all science teachers, although we have evidence that the form of public examinations profoundly affects practice in the lower secondary years, and particularly in year three. Since it is a policy at Arndale School to encourage movement from the bottom to the upper band at the end of the third year, it is necessary for pupils in both bands to cover some of the same content and to have assessment grades which are comparable. The solution arrived at was to design a core syllabus covering both bands, with syllabus extensions for the top band only. Understanding of the core syllabus is assessed by two tests during the year. The need to redesign a core syllabus which could be tackled well by the lower band pupils partly motivated the restructuring of the course.

A further important factor was the need for more detailed guidelines to be given to the non-specialist staff teaching biology to third year pupils in the school. It was felt that they needed more help with what to teach and, especially, how to teach it. The teacher responsible decided that the department's approach to 'A' level teaching (whereby pupils' specific weaknesses were diagnosed and remedial action then taken) could be emulated further down the school. By these means staff could more easily detect pupils' weak points and help individuals to reach the required standard. In this teacher's opinion both CSE biology and GCE biology syllabuses are becoming more technique-oriented and less concerned with simple factual recall. Hence, to succeed in the examinations, candidates need not only a thorough knowledge of the subject but also familiarity with different ways of presenting, using and interpreting that knowledge.

The list of examination skills in biology (Table 8) was drawn up from an analysis of examination syllabuses and past examination papers. In addition, discussions with other teachers at regional meetings (for CSE, Mode 1) was found to be helpful. A first draft of the list of skills was circulated to other science teachers in the school and their suggestions for clarification taken into account. The syllabus and the ten assessment exercises designed to monitor progress during the year were drawn up with the skills analysis specifically in mind. The pattern of teaching and assessment exercises is given in Figure 2 for the two bands. Mark schemes for the assessment exercises and arrangements for the collection and

Figure 2: **Third year biology course plan**

Pupils	Lessons	Assessments
All	1–18	Christmas exam. Easter exam. exercises 1–5
Top band only	19–34	Summer exam. exercises 6–10

Table 8: Arndale School's biology scheme of examination skills

EXAMINATION QUESTIONS SHOULD TEST KNOWLEDGE AND ONE OF THE FOLLOWING, OR MORE THAN ONE:

THE ABILITY TO

	1	2	3	4	5	6	7	8	9	10	Ø
Draw graphs				*†		*					
Interpret graphs			*†	*†		*					
Draw up tables		*†		*†		*					
Interpret tables		*†									
Draw diagrams from life or photos											*†
Compare diagrams			*†		*†						
Interpret diagrams		*†			*†						
Understand magnification		*†									
Draw a T.S. from an L.S.	*†	*†									
Understand written descriptions of new organisms	*†										
Understand written descriptions of new inter-relationships							*	*		*	
Explain adaptations											*†
Understand new experiments						*					
Interpret new experiments						*			*		
Explain experiment results						*					
Cope with simple maths				*†		*					
Criticize experiments				*†					*		
Design experiments (written not practical)						*			*		
Assessment Exercises (Short Teacher Tests)	1	2	3	4	5	6	7	8	9	10	Ø

Key: * Top band exercises
† Lower band exercises
Ø Classwork *must* include

collation from this were devised. Most of the tests concerned with the common core are very practical in nature.

This development is an example of a curricular change instigated hand-in-hand with a redesign of assessment procedures. Moreover, the assessment exercises were geared specifically to evaluate a key objective of the new course, namely the development of skills required for success in public examination work in biology. There is, therefore, an implicit acceptance by this department of the influence of the public examinations system and a determination to maximize their pupils' chances within it.

Summary of findings

Examinations

Periodic examinations taken by whole year groups remain the most common form of assessment that is recorded. In these cases, marking or grading tends to conform to a school-wide system. Contributions to such examinations generally come from all department members teaching the year group.

Influence of external examinations

External examination grading schemes become very influential by the third secondary year. Few departments check eventual examination performance against internal assessments made at this stage. Public examination syllabuses are generally regarded as a constraint in that teaching is channelled narrowly towards limited goals. Careful analysis of implicit objectives can, however, lead to a broadening of departmental assessment practices.

Influence of school policies

Although school policies often specified the grades to be used they less frequently specified their distribution or took account of the ability groupings within the school. Adoption of statistical procedures which enable proper comparisons to be made were rare.

Change

Heads of department tended to feel that change or improvement of assessment schemes should come from within and that working parties and consultation could best overcome reservations about acceptability of innovation or about increased work load.

External schemes

External assessment schemes such as LEA tests of graded objectives, published tests, etc. may be acceptable but their introduction and use should be given critical consideration for effects on staff, backwash on the curriculum and impact on the school's values, aims and assessment policies.

Meaning of assessment for pupils

Guidance for teachers on assessment was common at departmental level, but this tended to be limited to the style of test and mark scheme to be used. Few departments gave guidance on how marks could be interpreted for the benefit of pupils. Indeed, there was little evidence that departments spent time explaining the meaning of assessments to pupils. Very few schools were experimenting with pupil self-assessment.

Effort marks

Many schools now allocate 'effort' or 'progress' marks to widen their appraisals of pupils. The accuracy and relevance of these assessments remains in doubt; some teachers have objected on the grounds that they have little evidence with which to judge effort. Written comments sometimes contradicted the effort grade given, also there was an unwillingness to give high effort marks to academically low-achieving pupils.

Inter-curricular links

Some departments have forged curricular links but there is rarely any coordination on assessment of common material by teachers from different departments.

Assessment records

Pupil assessment records were almost entirely based on their written work. A small number of departments kept records made from informal observation or tests with a high practical or performance component.

Informal assessments

Informal assessments – those that do not contribute to final, recorded grades – are almost universally based on written work.

Agreed aims

Departments claimed agreed sets of aims more often than schools but had written them down less often.

Written departmental documents

Departments that used consultation were more likely to have formalized their outcomes in a written document about policies and procedures.

Chapter 4

Assessment in the Classroom

Introduction

The two preceding chapters focus on assessment policies and procedures at school and departmental levels. Results from the teacher questionnaire reported below add to the picture by describing assessment practices in the classroom. In addition, in this chapter we refer to two special studies on self-assessment. These are:

> A study of a pupil self-assessment in a 13+ comprehensive (Brampton School);
> A study of personal files in a secondary modern school (D.D. Deasey School).

It seemed likely that classroom practice may deviate from planned policies and guidelines (deviations for the good as well as the bad!) and that, for this reason, our survey should include some detailed questions to the teachers of 11–14-year-old pupils. In Chapter 5 we have examined selected schools using questionnaire data from all three levels in order to build up a picture of assessment policies and practices for individual schools. Some reference to this data is also made in this chapter.

The sample

Four hundred and sixty teachers responded from the twenty-seven schools. Only 12 per cent of the sample was from middle schools; these schools are of course much smaller and also, since they are typically organized by year group, not all staff teach the older (11,12 and 13–year-old) pupils.

In fact, 11 per cent of the total number of respondents reported that they taught within a year group and 88 per cent within a subject department. Two thirds of the sample taught more than one subject. This was more common amongst teachers of English, the humanities, physical and remedial education and commercial and business studies. We asked teachers who worked within a school organized into subject departments or faculties and who taught more than one subject to answer the questionnaire in the light of their main subject. Table 9 gives the main subject affiliation of respondents to the teachers' questionnaire and indicates that most subjects were adequately represented in the sample. Sixty-one per cent of the sample taught 11–12-year-olds, 67 per cent the 12–13-year-old group and 83 per cent taught 13–14-year-olds; many of the teachers, then, were concerned with the full 11–14-year-old age range.

Table 9: Teachers' sample: breakdown by subject

Main subject	No. questionnaires returned
Aesthetics and craft	77
Careers education	6
Commerce and business studies	6
English	59
Humanities other than English	58
Mathematics	63
Modern and classical languages	39
Physical education	30
Remedial education	19
Science	63
Social/community studies	2
Class teachers/general subjects teacher	36
Left blank	2
TOTAL	460

The questions, which asked about practices and purposes of assessment and about teachers' views on the subject, were almost all of the closed type. This eased data analysis but it did, unfortunately, mean that the results at this level lack the individual flavour afforded by open-ended responses. Some of the respondents evidently agreed. One teacher added this note at the end of his questionnaire:

I would much prefer not to have replied in yes/no terms, as I did not always do, in fact! So often I wished to answer 'yes/no but....', and what followed the 'but' would have given a fuller and more accurate answer.

Assessment practices in the classroom

For twenty-seven schools, data are available at the three levels of the survey and this gave us the opportunity to compare teachers' perceptions with those of heads of department and headteachers in the same school. These comparisons reveal that some schools are very much better than others at communicating school policy to class teachers. The main source of guidance for class teachers does seem to be the departmental or year group organization. We first compared what heads and teachers said about their school assessment policy documents. Heads were asked if a written assessment policy existed, and teachers whether they knew of such a document and had read it. Of the sixteen schools where answers could be compared, nine had a fairly large proportion of teachers who appeared to be misinformed. Overall, 38 per cent of teachers thought they had read a school policy document, when the head reported that this document did not exist. Further, in schools where school assessment documents did exist, 37 per cent of the teachers had not read them.

Generally, teachers were much better informed about their own departmental documents, and a fifth of the teachers had been involved in their development. Teachers expressed themselves reasonably satisfied with the guidance given by the school and department policies; 44 per cent thought enough guidance was given to fulfil school assessment requirements, whereas 63 per cent felt departmental guidance was sufficient.

However, the demands made of teachers were not particularly sophisticated, and usually consisted of a requirement to conform to a mark or grade system with a predetermined scale. Indeed, very few departments gave guidance as to how individual teachers might translate their assessments into the final scales which often appeared in records. There was evidence of a great variety of marking procedures. Clearly individual teachers enjoy considerable autonomy in making assessments for school or departmental purposes.

The methods used by teachers for processing marks were also investigated and the incidence of use of six procedures suggested in the questionnaire is given in Table 10.

Clearly, conversion of marks to both grades and percentages and the combining of test marks are common practices and many teachers also claim to distinguish between the various aspects of their subject when making assessments. The scaling of marks and the combining of marks from different subjects were less commonly practised. Further analysis showed that the majority of teachers used at least two, and in many cases three or four methods to process marks. Table 11 shows combinations of pairs of methods; thus, for example it indicates that 80 per cent of the 173 teachers who changed marks to a different scale also combined marks from different tests.

Table 11 indicates that a considerable amount of processing occurs in various ways. About the same use is made of grades and percentages (most teachers use both) and they are applied equally to the recording of different aspects of pupils' work. Although separate aspects of performance are frequently assessed, it is presumably likely that the grades or marks for these will be combined for some kind of summary record. The most appropriate method for combining marks (as discussed in Chapter 5) is conversion to a common scale with controlled distribution; a high proportion of teachers combine marks but only about half of these marks appear to be re-scaled. Combining assessments from several subjects is relatively rare. Some banding schemes do employ composite marks (often totalled over a limited range of academic subjects) and Table 11 shows that 21 of the 35 teachers who reported such inter-subject combinations did re-scale the assessments.

Table 10: Percentage of teachers using each method for processing marks

Method of processing marks	Percentage using method (n=460)
Recording marks to show performance on different aspects of the subject	69%
Converting marks to grades	67%
Converting marks to percentages	62%
Combining marks from different tests	58%
Changing marks to a different scale	38%
Combining marks from different subjects	8%

Table 11: Numbers and percentages of teachers using combinations of methods for processing marks

	Aspects	Scale	Combine	Grades	Percentages	Subjects
Aspects	316[†] (100%)	123 (39%)	205 (65%)	227 (72%)	207 (66%)	31 (10%)
Scale	123 (71%)	173[†] (100%)	139 (80%)	147 (85%)	136 (79%)	21 (12%)
Combine	205 (76%)	139 (52%)	269[†] (100%)	224 (83%)	215 (80%)	33 (12%)
Grades	227 (74%)	147 (48%)	224 (73%)	306[†] (100%)	227 (74%)	29 (9%)
Percentages	207 (73%)	136 (48%)	215 (76%)	227 (80%)	284[†] (100%)	26 (9%)
Subjects	31 (89%)	21 (60%)	33 (94%)	29 (83%)	26 (74%)	35[†] (100%)

Key

Aspects	=	Recording marks to show performance on different aspects of the subject
Scale	=	Changing marks to a different scale
Combine	=	Combining marks from different tests
Grades	=	Converting marks to grades
Percentages	=	Converting marks to percentages
Subjects	=	Combining marks from different subjects

† Teachers using each method. In each row the percentages are of these totals e.g. of the 173 teachers (100%) who scaled marks, 147 (85%) also converted to grades.

It is interesting to speculate on whether or not the bases for allocating and changing marks are made clear to pupils, particularly in view of the fact that teachers put much emphasis on the value of assessment for motivation purposes. Are pupils told, for example, if different skills within a subject are being assessed on different occasions? Do they know what a Grade B from a particular teacher means and, indeed, does it mean the same as a B from another teacher?

A further problem may arise with the procedures, such as the translation of marks from one scale to another, which require statistical treatments. Unfortunately, we know from answers to other questions that guidance on statistical procedures is minimal in most schools. The possibility of error and of distortion in the meaning of adjusted results must therefore be high.

Teachers were also asked how they compared marks or grades of pupils' performances – what bases of comparison were used? Did teachers compare work with an individual's previous performance or with that of other pupils in a group? Table 12 gives the results obtained.

Table 12: Percentage of teachers using various bases of comparison of attainment grades or marks

Comparison of pupil performance	Percentage using comparison (n=460)
Comparison with work done by others in the class	68%
Comparison with student's own work	63%
Comparison with work done by others in the year	54%
Comparison with work done by others in the band/stream	46%

It is interesting that 63 per cent of the teachers in this sample compare pupils' performances with the individual's previous work, though large numbers also make comparisons with other pupils. Many teachers clearly use marks or grades in two or more different ways, and Table 13 shows combinations of these.

Whilst comparison with classmates is the most prevalent base, teachers make frequent use of other comparisons with peers, to those in a pupil's band or year group. Table 13 indicates, for example, that 80 per cent of the teachers who compare the pupil's mark with his previous performance also compare that mark with those of other children in the class. These data raise interesting questions. How are both types of comparison made? Are they done on different occasions? Most importantly, how does the child interpret the assessment? Is the basis for comparison (or the dominant one) made clear to him?

Very few teachers in the sample were involved in introducing new assessment techniques into their departments, or developing existing

Table 13: Numbers and percentages of teachers using combinations of methods of comparison of marks or grades

	Student's own work	Others in the class	Others in the band	Others in the year
Student's own work	289[†] (100%)	230 (80%)	145 (50%)	145 (50%)
Others in the class	230 (73%)	314[†] (100%)	183 (80%)	178 (77%)
Others in the band	145 (68%)	145 (68%)	212[†] (100%)	156 (74%)
Others in the year	145 (59%)	178 (72%)	156 (63%)	247[†] (100%)

† Totals for teachers using each method, the percentages in each row are of teachers in this total using various combinations.

ones. The most common activities were the modification of examination papers (17 per cent of the sample), the development of methods of standardization between markers in a department (14 per cent) and the development of continuous assessment methods (11 per cent). Teachers may be involved in discussing these matters but this evidence suggests that very few appear to have direct responsibility for establishing new techniques or giving guidance to others.

Use of assessment in the classroom

In the questionnaire we suggested six possible uses to which assessments might be put and asked teachers to respond for the age groups they taught. Table 14 gives these results.

This evidence suggests that teachers have faith in the value of test results for motivating their pupils, although presumably other feedback methods, such as comments, operate and might well be considered to be more effective for this purpose. Mathematics, modern languages and humanities teachers were apparently more convinced of the encouraging effects of regular testing than teachers of English.

An impressive three-quarters of the teacher sample used assessment results as some kind of indication of their own effectiveness,

Table 14: Uses of classroom assessment

Uses of assessment	Age ranges		
	11–12 years (n=281)	12–13 years (n=308)	13–14 years (n=381)
Assessments used in order to create groups within the class based on ability	20%	16%	18%
Assessment results as the main method of giving feedback to students	52%	54%	56%
Regular testing as a means of encouraging students to work hard	62%	61%	64%
Assessments used as a means to judge the effectiveness of the teaching	77%	73%	77%
Assessment methods designed to prepare children for external examinations later in their school career	45%	54%	74%
Uses of grades or marks as a prediction of the courses the students will follow into external examinations	34%	44%	76%

though the precise form of this self-monitoring is not clear from the questionnaire. There was some evidence that teachers of aesthetics and craft and of physical education used assessments less than other teachers for this purpose.

Only relatively small numbers of teachers used assessment results to group pupils by ability within the class, though presumably in many cases they were already set or streamed. Again, there were some subject differences. More class teachers and remedial teachers organized groups of 11–12-year-olds by ability. From 12 years this was also true of mathematics teachers, and from 13 years, of foreign language teachers as well. Mathematics, science and foreign language teachers (and, from 13 years, careers teachers) were slightly more likely to use assessment results as their main method of feedback to students.

Predictably, the influence of external examinations on assessment of 11–14-year-olds was most strongly felt in the academic subjects, and increased sharply at 13–14 years. One teacher put it like this:

> It must be borne in mind that, as a pupil moves up the school, so the constraints imposed by the antiquated examinations systems we use become more influential in the assessment methods used.

Finally, consideration of the uses to which assessments are put in the classroom raises the question of whether teachers alone are in the best position to make these judgments. We encourage pupils to take responsibility for their own learning, but the right to assess that learning is rarely extended to them. Pupil perceptions of their attainment must surely be potentially useful for the purposes of informing both learning and teaching. This issue is discussed in the next section.

Who does the assessing?

Our survey of headteachers showed that results of self-assessment by pupils were included in school records of only six schools (six per cent of the sample). Yet we have encountered considerable interest in the subject on our visits to schools. It is almost as if many teachers and heads would like to introduce some measure of assessment of pupils by themselves, but they are unsure as to how to set about it. Indeed, in our teachers' survey, 22 per cent indicated that they would like to make more use of this method of assessment.

Two clearly distinct orientations can be identified in schools which do choose to involve pupils in assessment. In some schools personal files, compiled by pupils themselves, form the basis for summative reporting to outside agencies, particularly to prospective employers. We visited one school – D.D. Deasey – a secondary modern school where personal files were used by 14–16-year-old pupils and where the intention is now to start compiling these in lower years. The files contained a mixture of notes by the pupil (made during tutor periods) on such various topics as problems with particular subjects or teachers and descriptions of out-of-school activities and achievements. Attainment certificates were awarded by some departments – music and religious and physical education – and these were also included. Pupils whom we talked to obviously valued these certificates – perhaps an indication that they rated teachers' judgments of themselves higher than their own assessments. The clear orientation in this scheme, however, was towards prospective employers and it was success in this respect which seems to have convinced both staff and pupils of its usefulness. An extract from a letter sent to the head of the school illustrates one employer's views:

> One of these pupils brought along a personal profile which, he informed me, had been prepared at school, and which I found to be a very useful and informative document. I think the idea is excellent especially for pupils who, although they may have tried really hard, have a limited academic ability. I believe there are still many employers who are as impressed by honesty, integrity, keeness, punctuality and helpful attitude as they are by examination results.

> The object of writing to you is so that you may advise your boys and girls that this type of project is not a waste of time and effort, and is really a great help to employers.

Teachers stressed that employers were particularly impressed by testimonials from previous part-time employers (from paper-round jobs, etc.) contained in the files.

As another special study we visited Brampton, a small 13+ comprehensive school where pupils were involved in their own assessment. In this case the focus was on the classroom – the main purpose of pupil self-assessment being to give insights into the teaching and learning that pupils experienced. Pupils in the school write assessments of their progress in all subjects twice a year. They do this in class using an open form; that is, one which contains no specific questions. Teachers then write their reports, having read the self-assessment. With younger pupils only, these teachers' reports are sent home to parents. Two examples of pupil assessments (13-year-olds), together with teachers' reports, are given below.

Example 1: Peter

Student's report:

> I think that I am doing fairly well but still making a few mistakes with written work. I enjoy the discussions and like to join in on

them. We have been concentrating on science fiction and nuclear warfare. I found the reading and working on the crysalid very interesting and enjoyed it. I liked the work on Ray Bradbury. I have had problem with spelings. I would like to have both a comment and a mark, the comment to tell me where I gone wrong and the mark to see how I have got on.

Teacher's report:

Peter's approach to his work is mature and well organised. He makes an excellent contribution to discussion – or indeed to any other activity. He has a very positive influence on other members of the group and has the strength of character to pursue his own course. He has plenty of good ideas. Spelling does remain a weak point – he should make an effort to learn to spell words he repeatedly makes mistakes with – but apart from that written expression is good and his level of comprehension is high.

Example 2: Tim

Student's report:

The work has been quite easy and the homeworks have been quite easy to. I've only found learning the vocabularys a bit hard because I don't like sitting quiet and learning. I had oral German easy because you pronounce the words phonetically. I want to do 'O' level German. I don't spend a lot of time on learning because if I've written it, it is easier. I can't learn out of books.

Teacher's report:

Tim has made every effort to tackle the work in German so far, and seems able to assimilate new concepts in grammar without too much difficulty. As he himself admits, he could probably put a lot more effort into learning homeworks! His written work is of a good standard – although could be a little neater and orally he is very keen to have a try, whether or not he makes mistakes. A very encouraging sign!

From meetings with staff and students we identified several foci of interest and concern in this particular school. What were the intended purposes of pupil self-assessment, were these made clear to pupils and what uses were made of them? For whom were they written? Did pupils have adequate guidance on their composition?

We interviewed a small number of pupils in depth about their perceptions and value of self-assessment and also examined examples of written assessments. Results of these inquiries, together with discussion with staff, enabled us to draw some conclusions and to identify a few problems. The assessments seemed to be used for two main purposes – to inform the teachers of specific learning difficulties (aspects of a subject which either an individual or a group were finding problematic) and as a vehicle for pupil comment on the teaching. Pupils were convinced that teachers learnt about difficulties of which they were previously unaware. Several pupils said they preferred to write rather than to speak about these difficulties. One pupil explained, 'I think the teachers learn a lot about how you're coping because they don't have time to talk to everybody, so they get it from the assessments,' and a teacher concurred with this view, explaining that assessments 'Give you much more insight into individuals... it gives you something to pursue'.

The question of use of self-assessments as a means of commenting on teaching is of course a contentious issue. At Brampton we spoke to a probationary teacher who reported that he found pupil comments on his teaching methods extremely valuable; he had changed some aspects of his approach and some lesson content as a result. Pupils, too, instanced some positive outcomes of their critical comment on teaching. For example:

Interviewer: You mentioned commenting about teachers and teaching... do you use the reports in that way?

Pupil: Yeah... I did...because there was a teacher I wasn't particularly pleased with. I didn't think he was doing his best, so I wrote about that. Something did come of it...yeah...he's changed, changed a lot...

However, it must be said that the ethos of this school seemed conducive to a genuine sharing of responsibility for classroom learning and to such openness; the question of the use of self-assessments for comment on teaching may be much more problematic in other styles of school.

There was a tendency for pupils new to the school to write what they imagined teachers would like to read, but, as they became more used to the system, many pupils began to write for themselves. Some pupils said they would have no objection to parents seeing their self-assessments, but others disagreed. One girl explained that they were 'Something private between teacher and pupil'.

Staff found that most pupils made realistic and honest assessments of themselves. Unrealistic assessments could also be useful to the teacher. For example, it was not uncommon to identify pupils who were seriously underestimating their own capabilities. Interestingly, several pupils mentioned that they found it easier to write about problems than to write on aspects of subjects in which they were doing well.

Teachers explained that pupils needed careful guidance on how to write their self-assessments. Some of the pupils interviewed thought that headings and specific questions on the assessment form would be helpful. One pupil made the practical suggestion that examples of 'good' and 'bad' reports (that is, useful and not useful) would provide more specific help.

The overriding advantage of involving pupils in an assessment dialogue would seem to be that it provides insight into the effects of teaching – insight drawn from a thoroughly obvious and yet largely untapped source. By allowing pupils to take part in this dialogue their status as independent learners is acknowledged and under-lined. Indeed, we got the impression that pupils in this school both perceived and appreciated this fact. As one girl explained, '...they [the teachers] seem very keen on doing them you know, they make a lot of fuss about doing these self-assessments... they obviously think they're important'.

Whether the rather formal approach adopted in this school provides the ideal setting for this dialogue is perhaps open to question. Is there a danger that it might become a chore, a routine, a standard exercise?

We did visit one school in a different authority which is experimenting with 'pupil journals'. These are books in which the pupil can write anything at any time and the teacher responds when time allows. An extract from one of these journals is given below as an example.

Pupil entry

I don't really see the point of you setting us books to review of your choice as a homework. I would hope that in future you will let us review books of our own choice for homework.

R.S.V.P.

I don't see The Crucible as a very interesting book, it doesn't seem to have a real story. Why are we studying this book?

R.S.V.P.

Teacher's response

How do you choose books? What makes you choose a book to read? Is one way not to go on other people's advice? By all means I'll give you a chance to choose and review your own books.

Unfortunately, choice in literature is a matter of taste. What do you mean by a real story? Certainly something happens in the play doesn't it?

We are studying the book because it is set for the exam. I could choose from it or Shakespeare's 'Midsummer Night's Dream'. I thought you'd enjoy this more, but if you like I'll lend you a copy of M S N D to read and you can let me know what you think.

The intention is to avoid the artificiality, the 'plastic phrases' of report-writing, which tend to be used by both teachers and pupils. The obvious disadvantages of pupil journals, however, would seem to be that they must be extremely time-consuming for the teacher.

Despite considerable interest in the topic, then, instances of pupil involvement in assessment of their own leaning are relatively rare and it is for this reason that we have detailed some examples above.

Views on assessment in the classroom

Several questions on the questionnaire gave teachers an opportunity to express their views and opinions about assessment. For example, they were asked about their preferred marking or grading system, about the relative difficulty of assessing various aspects of pupil performance and about the importance they attach to a number of different assessment styles.

The view was expressed that no single marking or grading system was appropriate for all subjects and for children of all abilities. Several teachers advocated flexibility. For example, one teacher explained:

I prefer a mixture of systems. Too loose a system leaves pupils ill prepared for exam grading. Too tight a system can be destructive and narrowing.

Another teacher suggested that 'Different systems are applicable to different situations and types of work', and another wrote:

The essence of any assessment procedure must be to help the pupil. It is therefore necessary, on occasions, to utilize different methods to suit the personality of the pupil. No one method can achieve the desired results.

Of course, there is a danger that extreme flexibility would cause problems of interpretation – if different methods were applied to different individuals then inter-pupil comparisons would be inappropriate.

Thirty-six per cent of the teachers surveyed said that they had a preferred marking or grading system and 35 per cent gave details. These are summarized in Table 15.

Table 15: Preferred systems of marking or grading work

Preferred system	Percentage teachers (n=160)
Marks out of a predetermined total	31%
Mark/grade plus comment	22%
Grades alone	18%
Comment alone	17%
Others (including combinations of the above)	12%

Some teachers expressed the view that only a mark can give children a precise idea of their progress in relation to other pupils. The following remarks were made by teachers asked to explain their preferred marking system: 'Marking out of a predetermined number prepares students for the sort of assessment involved in public examinations in maths', and 'Children look for and compare marks. They rarely read comments'.

However, not all teachers agreed. Many preferred either a comment alone, or a comment in combination with a mark or grade. This method was particularly advocated by English and physical education teachers, and by class teachers in middle schools. The need to de-emphasize competition between pupils was given as one reason for this preference, as was the need to encourage pupils, particularly those of lower ability. One teacher explained, 'Questions can be either right or wrong. Comments are vital to show why they are wrong. Conversely they encourage good work.' One teacher thought that 'Comments with no grades encourage lower ability pupils whereas poor performance continually in a graded system discourages them'. Another teacher discussed the advantages for himself of recording assessments in the form of comments and explained:

> In order to facilitate writing reports, references, 'court reports' and assessments for other interested parties, I keep a record of each pupil in my mark book but in the form of comments (not marks). This is very useful and often more informative than the marks.

Most teachers felt that some aspects of pupil performance were inherently more difficult to assess than others. Motivation, creativity and personality characteristics were considered to be the most difficult. Only a fifth of the sample thought that assessment of written expression was problematic, whereas more than half thought spoken expression to be so. Fourteen teachers cited aspects of performance which were not specified on the questionnaire as being particularly difficult to assess. These included the assessment of attitudes, of manipulative and other physical skills, of higher order thinking (e.g., whether ideas were grasped, concepts linked, etc.), and of pupil potential. The difficulty of diagnosis and assessment of physical problems of any sort was also mentioned.

Finally, teachers were asked to express their opinions on the styles of assessment they would prefer rather than on their current practices. In the questionnaire a variety of methods was listed and teachers were asked to rate these on a three-point scale which was explained in the following way: *Essential* meant that it was absolutely necessary to gain a proper picture of the student; *Important* indicated that the form of assessment was important but could be left out without distortion of an evaluation of an individual's ability. *Unnecessary* is self-explanatory. Four types of assessment were designated *Essential* by more than 50 per cent of the sample, as shown below.

Essential – end of year examinations;
measures to show change in individual performances;
continuous assessment of classwork;
marks or grades for effort.

Nearly half the teachers also thought it essential to make informal assessments of student behaviour. Pupil self-assessment and assessment of project work were seen as most inessential (although for both these categories nearly half the teachers felt they were *Important*).

Three types of assessment were viewed as *Unnecessary* by more than half the respondents as shown.

Unnecessary – regular termly (or more frequent) examinations;

continuous assessment of essay writing;

pupil self-assessment.

Some assessment styles were considered to be *Important*. The high percentage figures here seemed to occur for those aspects of assessment which are either currently in vogue or particularly difficult to execute (because techniques are poorly developed). These are given below – they probably represent styles and methods which are practised far less than they are preached.

Important – the use of tests to indicate achievement of a predetermined standard;

the assessment of aspects of oral ability;

continuous assessments based on objective style tests;

the use of diagnostic tests;

the use of independent assessors for comparison of marks or grades.

Forty-one per cent of the sample considered standardized tests (to enable comparison with national standards) to be *Unnecessary*, while 12 per cent thought this was *Essential* and 47 per cent thought it *Important*. Of course, standardized tests are available for only a small range of the subjects taught i.e., concerning only about one third of the teachers in the sample; in this context the proportions considering their use essential or important are high.

Some issues arising

It is clear from results in this chapter that not all schools communicate policy on assessment as well as they think they do. In some schools, teachers are obviously unaware of guidelines laid down in those policies.

Important judgments about children's progress are based on results of assessments, yet it does seem that there is often insufficient consideration of the value and purposes of these assessments. A mark (or grade) is the most common form of feedback to the individual pupil. It thus carries a heavy load of meaning. Is this meaning always communicated and understood? Does the pupil know how the mark was awarded, and for what? These are important questions for teachers who believe that future learning and motivation are influenced by assessment results.

A recognition of pupils as learning partners leads to the notion of involving them in assessment of aspects of their work. Teachers apparently value assessment as a means of improving classroom learning and teaching – pupil self-assessment seems one promising way of contributing to such an improvement.

Chapter 5

Issues, Problems and Possible Solutions

Introduction

This final chapter is organized into four fairly distinct sections. They appear together because they represent key issues and problems which have emerged from our research, and recommendations which follow from them. The first three sections explore different areas which many practitioners find problematic. The first of these is general and philosophical, the second organizational and the third technical. In the fourth section we make some practical suggestions for schools embarking on an assessment review. These four concluding sections are organized as shown below.

(A) Purposes and meanings of assessment

In almost all schools with 11–14-year-old pupils, assessment results are used to make important decisions about children's lives. The relationship between methods and purposes of assessment is explored and the question of interpretability of assessment results raised.

(B) Organizational issues exemplified by outline descriptions of assessment policies and practices in three schools

Pen-portraits of assessment in three 11–18 comprehensive schools in our sample illustrate the range of existing practice and raise important practical questions of organization which LEAs and schools need to resolve.

(C) Technical issues associated with processing and interpretation of results

Teachers compare and combine marks and allocate grades for attainment and effort. The processes whereby these are achieved need to be free from gross technical error.

(D) Pointers to good practice

On the recommendation of our Advisory Group, as well as of heads and teachers who took part in the study, some research conclusions are translated into practical suggestions for schools.

The chapter ends with a few summarizing remarks.

(A) Purposes and meanings of assessment

A range of purposes

The notion of purposes seems to us to be crucial. It is no exaggeration to say that for some (many?) teachers, assessment is put to no effective use other than to discriminate between children. There is nothing wrong with group comparisons; comparisons within classes, sets and years and from year to year can provide valuable feedback on general trends and on the relative progress of individuals. But they do not fulfil all the purposes of assessment which teachers say they value. Comparison of the performances of individual pupils (against their previous performances), evaluation of teaching success and reflection on the suitability of the material taught are all valid purposes of assessment which many teachers acknowledge and aspire to.

Are the methods of assessment which are adopted in practice, however, sufficiently varied and sufficiently realistic to meet these different purposes? It seems not. Our evidence suggests that the matching of appropriate methods to purposes (or intentions) is haphazard. Most attention is focused and energy expended on methods – that is, on how assessment is carried out and on the formal trappings of recording and reporting. There are few attempts to link these very important issues (the 'how' questions) with the even more fundamental "value" questions of intention (the 'why' questions). Our special study of the development of school assessment policy at Woodvale School (Chapter 2) illustrates the inseparability of assessment methods and educational purposes, once this connection is recognized.

Specific purposes might range from the monitoring of a particular learning problem in a child over a period of time to a global assessment of mastery of some basic facts by a group of children. It is unlikely that the same method could cope adequately with these disparate purposes. Yet how often is the issue of appropriateness tested by asking: 'Do the methods of assessment fulfil the specific intended purposes?'

If this question were addressed more rigorously it seems likely that a poor matching of method and purpose would often be revealed. Perhaps then, radical questions about methods would arise. Our study generally showed considerable uniformity in assessment practice. The great majority of assessments of pupil performance are made on the basis of written work, for example, and the majority of recorded results consists of marks or grades awarded for formal tests or examinations. But at the same time teachers' comments on the questionnaires showed that they are not happy with this situation and have little faith in these methods.

Nearly half of the departmental heads surveyed said that they would aim to use assessments as a basis for reviewing teaching practice in their departments. Yet we know that in only a very few schools are pupils (whether they are viewed as clients of a process or partners in it) allowed any opportunity to comment formally on their own learning and therefore, presumably, on the success of the teaching. The experience of pupil self-assessment at Brampton School, reported in Chapter 4, suggests that pupils are indeed a most valuable source of information – yet it is one which most teachers ignore.

A range of methods

When teachers do broaden the range of activities which they assess, to include aspects other than formal written work, they are frequently surprised (and sometimes delighted) by their pupils' performances. The following description of one middle school teacher's attempts to extend her usual range of assessment methods illustrates this. This teacher was a member of a group with which we worked on the development of assessment in 'topic' work. She had previously relied on the commonly-used method of marking and commenting on 'folders' handed in at the end of the topic. The main criterion for this assessment is usually the general standard of presentation. She experimented with a variety of alternative approaches, including attention to children's oral contributions and their interpretation of maps, drawings and pictures. She also posed some 'naive' questions for immediate written response by her pupils without special regard for presentation, etc. For example, she asked them, after several introductory lessons, to write about why they thought they were going on a visit to a Victorian industrial museum (the topic was based around this visit). One girl, judged by the teacher to be able, wrote: 'Because in social studies we are doing about Saxons and Normans and we are doing about Iron and Steel for swords and shields'. It turned out that she had assumed that the topic was a continuation of the previous one, which was about the medieval period! Another girl, however, whose written explanations were usually very poor, and who was considered by the teacher to be a 'remedial' pupil, wrote the following: 'Because it is interesting to find out how indosery stared in Sheffield'.

Here is the teacher's reflection on these experiments:

> The assessment was most useful in pointing out the inaccuracy of my overall mental impression of the level of the understanding of the class and provided a map of their ideas and misconceptions. Also, I was able to identify gaps in my own teaching, things I had assumed they had grasped, with little foundation for my assumption.
>
> Through examining their responses I was able to identify progress and good understanding in later work. I became more perceptive about each individual's progress and capabilities.

Finally, she concluded:

> I decided that the written method of assessment of topic work was rather biased toward those with good literacy skills and perhaps not always reflective of the true state of affairs. I feel, therefore, that it is still important to structure the work of, and give challenging tasks to, those poor at presentation, rather than simply providing them with remedial-type resource material.
>
> The exercise improved my motivation and sense of purpose in the work and this carried over to the class. There was always a desire to identify our aims and clarify what we meant. Many of the children began to organize their work in a fairly structured way using sections and sub-headings.

The point of giving this example at length is to illustrate how, when teachers are encouraged to think about purposes, they find it necessary to draw on a wider range of assessment techniques. Of course, though some of these 'techniques' may be extremely inexact or poorly developed when used at first, they may nevertheless prove highly indicative (i.e., valid, to use the technical term).

Assessment of children's oral work, for example, is very difficult in this respect. We found that very few departments and schools assessed oral performance (apart from the use of oral and listening tests in modern language teaching), perhaps because it is so difficult. Most categorical schemes (where aspects of oral contributions – such as fluency, ability to switch register, ability to frame appropriate questions, etc. are separately assessed according to certain criteria) are notoriously cumbersome, impracticable for a teacher to use and often ultimately unsatisfactory in the quality of information they yield. Yet we have evidence from the development work on 'topic work' referred to above that teachers find it extremely worthwhile simply to focus their attention on children's oral contributions (by listening carefully, by sometimes taping talk and by recording their impressions gleaned). The point is that it is not only well-developed, exact, 'scientific' techniques which can yield useful information; indeed 'rough and ready' or more reflective methods may be just as valuable.

Meanings of assessment results: do the pupils understand?

To return to the question of purposes, a major reason for their non-fulfilment would seem to be that, even if methods of assessment were appropriate, the link back to the purpose would not be forged. It is assumed to occur automatically. Thus, although our evidence indicates that teachers believe in the usefulness of assessments as feedback to pupils, they do not routinely explain the meaning of the assessment results they give. We know that many teachers give marks or grades without comment to individual pupils, that they use different criteria on different occasions and that a number of different bases of comparison may be used in arriving at grades. Are pupils told, for example, if an essay is being marked mainly for narrative development or for grammatical accuracy? Does the teacher explain that this week a homework mark is awarded by comparison with last week's performance, whereas on another occasion individual performances are compared to the rest of the group? Teachers have faith in the value of feedback, particularly in the motivating effects of assessing work. Indeed, there is evidence from evaluation of tests of graded objectives, such as that reported in Chapter 3, that pupils under certain circumstances *are* motivated. It may be, however, that often purposes remain frustrated because too little attention is devoted to explaining the meaning of assessments to precisely those people who are most concerned.

Meanings to those outside the classroom

Non-communication of meanings occurs as well outside the class-room. At school level, teachers need to understand the value of others' assessments. This is particularly necessary where agreed common procedures do not exist.

The meanings and value of assessment results given to parents and governors are frequently left unexplained. For example, it may not be made clear which set or band a child is in. If examination marks are unscaled they are not comparable, but it is likely that many parents will assume that marks of 85 per cent for geography and 73 per cent for history 'mean' that the child is better at geography than history. We know from our survey that there is little statistical treatment of results in order to compare marks. It seems to us that this question of inter-subject comparability is extremely important and is relatively easily solved. In the third section of this chapter we outline simple graphical methods for scaling marks. We drew on the experience of a comprehensive school in our sample where such methods are being developed. The concern in this school was to arrive at a method which is simple, not time-consuming and easily understandable to non-mathematicians.

When assessment results are passed between schools their meanings may also be distorted. It is not usual, for example, for secondary schools to receive comparable test results from their feeder primary schools. Examples of standardization on this, such as that operating at Highfield School outlined in Chapter 2, are rare.

These problems of communication raise important issues for schools. How can accurate transfer of information be facilitated? How can schools ensure that planned change is implemented? To illuminate these and other questions we selected three schools of similar type and size (all 11–18 comprehensives with rolls between 1500 and 1650) from our survey. The three outlines given in the next section are an overview of policy and practice in these schools. Data from all three types of questionnaire were drawn on for evidence to support the arguments.

(B) Organizational issues: assessment policy and practice in three school

The sketches are not offered with value-laden comparisons in mind, for our work indicates quite clearly that there are no single, right answers; that approaches which work for one school are not necessarily appropriate for another.

Table 16 shows the numbers of questionnaires returned from the three schools. Data for the three sketches were obtained from questionnaires but in fact we also made visits and had personal contacts in two of these schools (A and C) and these impressions

**Table 16: Numbers of questionnaires returned from
three schools**

School	Headteacher questionnaire	Head of department questionnaire	Teacher questionnaire
(A) Baltham	✓	15 (71% return)	61 (71% return)
(B) Hill Top	✓	15 (60% return)	36 (55% return)
(C) Grange	✓	19 (73% return)	37 (55% return)

supported the accounts. School (C), Grange, changed from a grammar to a comprehensive school in 1959 yet, in the opinion of senior staff, assessment procedures had changed little over that period. The school now intends to embark on a radical review.

School (A): Baltham School

This school has a written school policy on assessment which is under continual development. A deputy head has special responsibility for coordination of assessment (for policy-making and review) and convenes regular meetings. Replies from the heads of department indicate that he plays an active role and offers a variety of advice, including explanation of policy and detailed guidance on the statistical procedures to be adopted. The school policy deals both with relating individual performances to that of the year group, and with the assessment of effort. The policy also determines methods of record keeping, the standardization of marks to enable inter-subject comparability and cross-year comparisons and the combination of results of continuous assessment with those of periodic assessments. All heads of department except for P.E. and special education said that their departmental policies were determined by school policy and the influence was specific, as one response made clear:

> School assessment policy determines department policy. Each pupil's attainment is assessed on a 1–5 (norm referenced, grade 1=10 per cent, grade 2=20 per cent, grade 3=40 per cent etc.) and their effort on an A–E descriptive scale.

A minimum of two such common assessments is required each year by the school. How the attainment grades are allocated is left to departments, as one head of department explained: 'Our department arrives at these grades via a numerical procedure involving exams, set tasks and assessed class work'.

There is considerable intra-departmental conformity as well – within the majority of departments (80 per cent), all members use the same mark or grade system. This fairly uniform pattern is confirmed by examination of teachers' questionnaires from selected departments. Teachers in the English department award grades (on a five-point scale) and frequently supplement the grade with comment. The science and mathematics departments, by contrast, award marks out of predetermined totals.

Statistical treatments of departmental results are quite common with, for example, a third of departments calculating means, standard deviations and producing distribution graphs. Seven arts and humanities departments are involved in some kind of statistical adjustment and presentation of assessment results. For example, the history department produces distribution graphs and scaled marks, calculates standard deviations and analyses individual question results.

School (B): Hill Top

At first glance the organization of assessment procedures at Hill Top looks rather similar to that just described. The school has a written policy which deals with grading guidelines for attainment (an A–E scale) and effort (a 1–5 scale) and with record keeping. There is no standardization of marks in the central school records.

However, only some of the science departments and the European studies department report that their policies are determined by this school policy. Large departments, such as English, mathematics and technical subjects reported no such influence and a closer look at the open-ended responses suggested that the concerns of school policy were limited, in effect, to school examinations. One departmental head explained that 'formal assessment is school policy, departmental is separate'.

The school has a coordinator in charge of assessment, but only half the departmental heads appeared to know of his existence! Replies from others indicated that his influence was limited. He acted as 'a preliminary source of information about incoming pupils', and provided 'guidance on how forms etc. should be filled in', and issued 'occasional instruction sheets'.

However, the majority of departmental heads reported that all members within their department used the same mark or grade system. The exceptions are the English and music departments. In this school there is clearly much departmental autonomy. Departmental results are, as at Baltham, subjected to a variety of statistical procedures, with a third of the departments calculating means and standard deviations and producing graphs of distribution. However, there is no evidence that the arts and humanities departments use these methods; it is the mathematics, science and technical results which are treated in these ways.

Again, teachers in the science and mathematics departments preferred to award marks out of predetermined totals but descriptions of preferred mark/grade systems from four English teachers illustrate the diversity of practice in this department:

Marks out of a predetermined total. Makes pupils aware of their progress plus the idea of competitiveness. Also effort to be assessed.

Comment plus marks – the children like to have a mark but a comment can be used to encourage those with low marks and suggest how they can improve.

Generally, marks out of a predetermined total because, contrary to most educational opinion, children do like to know how they are assessed and how they rate in comparison with other children.

I prefer to comment with no grade system because it prevents too much emphasis on competition whilst allowing encouragement or criticism to be made.

Thus, although Baltham and Hill Top schools are superficially similar, there are some significant differences. At Baltham, the school policy practically influences departmental and classroom practice and this influence is carefully monitored and controlled. The statistical treatment of assessments in non-mathematical subjects bears witness to the level of standardization in the school. At Hill Top school, policy influence appears to be weak and the 'unit' of organization of assessment procedures is the department. Within most departments, however, there is considerable standardization of practice.

School (C): Grange
The third school stands in contrast to both the previous examples. This school's assessment policy, which deals with pupils' perform-

ances in relation to their teaching groups, with pupil effort and with record-keeping, is not written down. Central records contain only results of multiple-choice tests. Five heads of department (26 per cent) reported some influence from school policy – this related to school examinations, as one response made clear: 'We conform to the pattern of internal examinations'.

Only two departmental heads and two deputy heads were aware that the school had a member of staff with responsibility for coordination of assessment and the following response indicates that his brief is limited:

The responsibility of the person does not extend to (b) [giving help and advice]. The examinations assessment is merely collected on a sheet and actions taken when patterns emerge.

In six departments teachers used the same mark/grade system but the rest (68 per cent) had no such intradepartmental consensus. Clearly a majority of teachers in this school formulated their own individual assessment scheme, a conclusion confirmed by examination of the teacher questionnaires.

Few departments in this school carried out any statistical treatment of their results. The exception was the physics department which performed detailed analyses.

Concluding remarks

The three examples make an interesting set and suggest a wide variety of practice in schools similar in type and size. At Baltham, assessment procedures are highly, though not rigidly, structured from the top. Generally, communication within the school seems efficient – teachers know about assessment policies and their implications. The deputy in charge of assessment carefully monitors implementation. At Hill Top, responsibility for assessment is devolved to departmental level, where in most cases clear guidelines for practice exist and are followed. At Grange, it is mostly individual teachers who have had to devise their own schemes of practice.

Issues raised

What issues and problems do these descriptions raise? Is it advantageous to write down assessment policy guidelines? What are the factors which facilitate the translation of policies into plans of action? Is it necessary for assessment to be co-ordinated in some way at the level of the school or of the department? How is change best effected? What are the constraints on the implementation of innovation?

WRITTEN POLICIES

Whether assessment policies are written down is, of course, a matter of management style. For smaller middle schools such formality might not be necessary and could fit badly with the ethos of the school. For larger schools a written document may be advisable, if not indispensable. Although policy ideally starts with a consideration of purposes, and essentially this ought to be made very explicit, this alone is not adequate. The policy needs translation into a plan; a clear plan of action to be communicated throughout the school.

COORDINATORS FOR ASSESSMENT

Two-thirds of the schools with written policies had a member of staff responsible for coordination of assessment. Is this an important factor? Only 39 per cent of schools in our sample had such a post-holder and we know that their most usual function was the supervision of translation of departmental marks to school grades. It is also clear that where the teacher concerned plays an active role, and performs a variety of functions, as at Baltham School, there is good communication of policy and consistency of procedures. Even in schools with established policies, much maintenance work is required. This would probably include induction of new members of staff, organization of school-based in-service programmes, provision of technical and statistical advice (including use of microcomputers), as well as a general coordinating function to ensure that policy decisions are implemented throughout the school. The large number of teachers who reported ignorance of the very existence of their coordinator for assessment suggests that in many schools the impact is low.

UNDERSTANDING THE VALUE OF ASSESSMENT: CONSULTATION

We think that it is untrue that teachers are not interested in assessment. Where there is demonstrable benefit to pupils, to teaching methods or to curricular planning – where teachers can see the value of their efforts – they do consider it worthwhile. They are justifiably mistrustful of time spent on assessment if the (often thinly) veiled purpose is seen to be jumping on a band-wagon, or simply to achieve a variety of administrative or organizational changes. For example, long, complicated pupil profile forms ought to be useful to the teacher (and to the pupil) and not merely a fashionable innovation to impress the outside world.

Our study supports the idea that consultative procedures, both to decide on change and to implement it, are the most effective. This seems to be so both at school and departmental levels. School-based in-service courses seem one good way of encouraging full teacher participation. Teachers must feel that they understand the change – the reasons for it, its organization and its intended benefits. Many of our examples of innovatory practice were in schools where thorough consultation had occurred. This was true, for example, for the development of school policy at Woodvale (Chapter 2), the continued implementation of pupil self-assessment at Brampton (Chapter 4) and the coordination of assessment in a pyramid of schools at Highfield (Chapter 2).

TIME: THE MAIN CONSTRAINT ON CHANGE

Time is an important constraint on change and must remain a major consideration for heads and management teams. However, it should be said that some changes may result in time saving. There is no doubt that if microcomputers can be used to process assessment data, then not only is more valid information about pupil performance obtained but teacher time can be saved. Some very successful innovations have, however, increased time spent on assessment. For example, graded tests in modern languages, and now in mathematics, seem to be increasingly popular with teachers. Here new assessment procedures are linked with curricular innovation. They are essential for the achievement of one of the main purposes of the change – direct, regular feedback to individual pupils as a motivation for further learning (and as a pat on the back for effort already made). The point to emphasize is that here considerable extra time spent on pupil assessment is deemed valuable and, under these circumstances, many teachers are happy to give it.

(C) Technical issues associated with the processing and interpretation of results

Introduction

At certain points in a pupil's school career it is most important for schools to have high quality procedures for processing marks or grades. Because of this we include here a section which expands the comments made in Chapters 2 and 3 about the processing of marks and describes some common problems and simple methods of avoiding the worst pitfalls.

These technical aspects matter whenever marks or grades are combined for the purposes of reporting and record keeping. They are important, too, when a pupil's assessment results in different subjects are compared at the end of the third secondary year (at 14+) when option choices are made, and also when pupils are compared to make up subject sets. Proper comparison can only be made when marks are based on a common scale, otherwise they may be misleading. Teachers' idiosyncratic mark patterns account for much variation in score distributions.

Comparing scores: variations in patterns

HARD AND LENIENT MARKERS

One problem is the level of severity of marking, since some markers habitually give higher scores than others. A method of checking on this is to compare the average marks given by each teacher. The scripts or exercises from pupils awarded marks nearest to the common average can then be appraised to see whether there are grounds for adjusting marks or re-marking.

Another reference point would be the middle mark of the range of scores provided by the mark scheme. If, for example, the middle point of the mark scheme is 30 and the average marks for two teachers are 55 and 45, then the teacher with the average of 55 might be regarded as unduly lenient. In this case, pupils with a mark nearest to each teacher's average would be appraised to see whether the difference could be substantiated. Also in this instance, all scripts awarded 45 or thereabouts could be compared to guide moderation. Of course, the mid-point of a mark scale has no particular merit other than convenience for judging whether the marks awarded have been biased.

Any differences between markers would have to support consistently the acknowledged differences between groups of pupils. Some of these difficulties might be avoided if 'agreement trials' are held before the bulk of scripts is marked. But the follow-up checks would be just as necessary. Variations between teachers would show most clearly if two teachers were to mark the same set of scripts.

The object is to prevent the superficial comparison of marks which might lead an uninformed person, a parent or teacher, to assume that the higher mark really meant better attainment. For example, if two teachers award marks of 74 and 64 to the same pupil, but the average mark from the second teacher is 20 points lower (for the same group of pupils), the mark of 64 might well indicate the better relative attainment. If option choices are involved and biased marks given in separate subjects remain uncorrected, then a false choice could occur. The mean mark of the set of scores awarded by each teacher is, therefore, worth considering when comparing pupils' marks.

DIFFERENCE IN THE SPREAD OF MARKS

The previous example indicated that the amount by which a pupil's score deviates from the mean score can be critical. Also when teaching groups are considered, the spread of marks in each set may be quite substantial but different for each set. This is important when marks are combined. The pattern of marks can be studied by observing the way they are spread on either side of the average mark (i.e., arithmetic mean) of the group. One indicator of this dispersion is the 'standard deviation'. Table 17 shows how examination data might look for one (fictional) pupil in three subjects.

Table 17: Test marks expressed as proportion of standard deviation for corresponding sets of marks

Subject	Standard deviation of marks for sets in each subject	Pupil's exam mark	Average (mean) of marks in subject	Difference between mark and mean	Proportion of standard deviation
Biology	10	60	50	10	10/10=1.0
Chemistry	15	60	50	10	10/18=0.66
Physics	20	60	50	10	10/20=0.5

In Table 17, only the spread of marks has been varied, with the difference between pupil's mark and class mean score kept the same at 10 points. In relation to the dispersion of marks in each subject set the pupil has done best in biology and least well (not necessarily badly) in physics. For school examinations or homework totals, the teaching set mean scores will probably be different, for instance, as in Table 18. At first sight this pupil appears to have performed best

Table 18: Data for one pupil in three subjects

Subject	Standard deviation of marks for sets in each subject	Pupil's exam mark	Average (mean) of marks in subject	Difference between mark and mean
Biology	18.0	68	50.5	17.5
Chemistry	14.4	56	41.8	14.2
Physics	17.2	63	43.0	20.0

in biology. However, the mean is highest for biology and this has the biggest standard deviation (i.e., the biggest spread). In biology and chemistry, the difference between the pupil's mark and the mean is almost equal to the respective standard deviations, whilst in physics the mark differs from the mean by more than the standard deviation value. Assuming that the same group of pupils took all three subjects, then physics was the pupil's best result. The mark of 63 represents $^{20}/_{17.2} = 1.16$ standard deviations. For the other subjects the ratios are $^{17.5}/_{18} = 0.97$ (biology) and $^{14.2}/_{14.4} = 0.99$ (chemistry). The standard deviation is an average based upon the difference between the mean mark (i.e., average for a given set of pupils) and each pupil's mark, as shown in the final column of Table 18. Clearly, pupils below the average would show negative differences, but the values for each pupil are then squared (all signs are positive) and these are summed. This 'sum of squares' is divided by the number of pupils in the set to give the average squared deviation. The square root of this figure is the standard deviation for the set of marks.

Nowadays computers make very easy the transformation of scores to deviation scores, as shown above. Because any pupil with a mark below the average for his set would receive a negative score, it is usual to fix an arbitrary mean at, say 50, and to add or subtract, say, ten times the deviation score. For example, a pupil with -1.5 deviation score would receive $50 - 15 = 35$ as a scaled score.

Combining scores

A number of schools in our sample added marks and some staff had noticed that certain subjects influenced combined marks more than others. The effect of different ranges when scores are combined is illustrated by the following hypothetical example. Table 19 shows the top and bottom of score lists for 30 pupils in two subjects (A and B). A comparison of these shows that the teacher for B used a narrower range of marks. When the two sets are added and

**Table 19: High and low ends of scores for thirty pupils
in two subjects**

Pupil	Subject 'A'	Subject 'B'	Average 'A & B'	
1st	44	34	39	
2nd	42	32	37	High
3rd	40	30	35	end
4th	38	28	33	
				Middle scores omitted
27th	14	20	17	
28th	12	20	16	Low
29th	8	16	12	end
30th	6	10	8	
Range of scores	38	24	31	

Note: this illustration is artificial in that only rarely would a group of
pupils produce the same rank order in two examinations.

averaged, marks from A tend to dominate the eventual order. It can
be seen that pupils' marks which are tied in teacher B's marking
become separated after combination. In some cases (e.g., those
pupils in 3rd and 4th positions) an order of merit is created in line
with that in subject A. This example shows that teachers who use a
wide range of marks in a mark scheme (in this case teacher A) have a
greater effect on final combined scores than those who use only a
narrow range.

The pattern of marks for the whole group in Table 19 can be
presented graphically. Figure 3 shows clearly how the patterns
differ. For subject A the distribution is much wider than for subject
B.

By giving each set of marks the same central point and dispersion,
a standard scale can be created whereby the mean and spread are
fixed. This serves two important purposes – firstly, it ensures that
marks can be combined without incidentally changing the correct
order of merit and secondly, differences of severity and breadth of
marking are balanced out. The spread can be fixed by deciding
(arbitrarily) on the size of the scaled standard deviation (SD). The

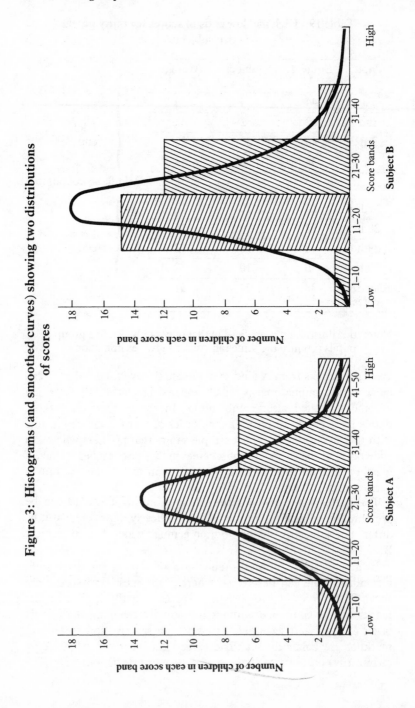

Figure 3: Histograms (and smoothed curves) showing two distributions of scores

larger the SD the wider will be the final standardized spread of scores. All teachers' marks could be scaled in this way, which would mean they were comparable across subjects, but pupils' order of merit within each subject would remain the same.

For combining marks, then, the important aspect is spread of scores. The means obtained by groups of pupils in different subjects do not have to be identical (as the difference between them amounts to a constant for each pupil in relation to their deviation from the mean). To calculate means and standard deviations with the aid of microcomputers the data need only be typed in according to program specification. Some schools had written their own programs and these not only standardized sets of marks and produced graphs but compiled record files for storage on discs or print-outs. For those without computer facilities, and for those who are interested to see roughly what happens in score transformations, practical graphical procedures are described below.

Two scaling methods

(i) SAME MEAN AND SD

A simple scaling method is one which uses a graph based on three points. Figure 4 shows how this was constructed in one of our schools using data from one subject examination. The mean and standard deviation were calculated for the teacher's set of marks; these were plotted against a standard scale. First (stage A), the raw marks were set out along the bottom axis showing a mean of 50.3 and one SD above (SD for these marks was 18.5) at 68.8 and one SD below at 31.8. For stage B, the vertical axis is the standard scale with the mean set at 50 and an SD set at 15 (+1 SD is at 65, therefore, and −1 SD is at 35). The three intersecting points were found and a straight line drawn through them. In stage C, each pupil's mark was standardized by reading from the horizontal axis to the vertical axis.

(ii) FIXED SCORE-BAND PROPORTIONS

Another method uses percentiles which are based upon the percentages of pupils achieving certain scores. In looking at a range of marks it is possible to count how many pupils there are between zero and any mark chosen. The number counted is then expressed as a percentage of those tested altogether. In this method several percentile positions are selected from the raw scores and plotted against a standard scale.

Figure 4: Stages in constructing a score standardization chart

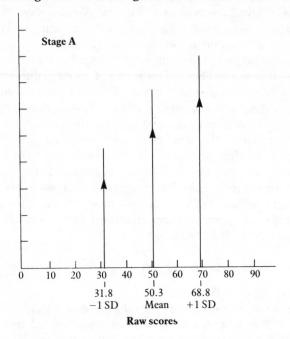

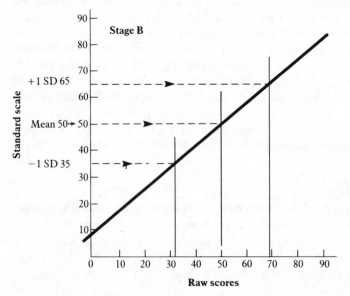

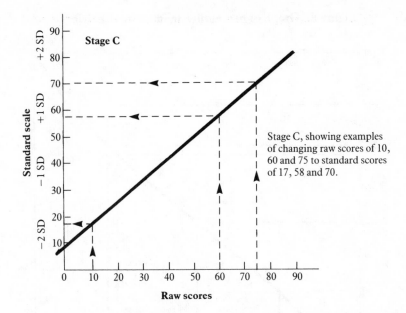

Stage C, showing examples of changing raw scores of 10, 60 and 75 to standard scores of 17, 58 and 70.

For example, if three pupils in a set of 30 scored 7 or less in a test, then 1/10 or ten per cent of the pupils would have been counted. A score of seven would then be at the tenth percentile of that range of marks. Clearly, the score obtained by the pupil half-way up the rank order is the 50th percentile (or the median). In this procedure, pupils within a given percentile band are awarded scores within a sector of the standard scale chosen. The sectors dividing the standard scale are decided on arbitrarily. In the illustration which follows the standard score and percentile points have been paired as shown in Figure 5. It has been decided that 25 per cent of pupils' scores will fall between 50 and 70 on the standard scale, 15 per cent between 70 and 85 and the top 10 per cent will receive more than 85 marks and conversely below the mid score point, as tabulated below.

standard score	15	30	50	70	85
percentile	10th	25th	50th	75th	90th

In contrast to the previously described method, where each teacher's raw scores would produce a certain mean and SD, this method starts with the particular percentile points arising from marks awarded by each teacher. It tends to smooth out irregularities

Figure 5: Graph of percentile/standard mark pairings

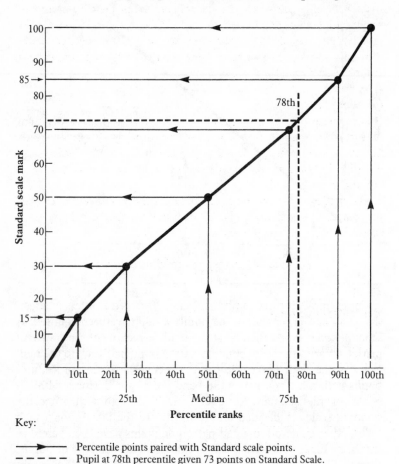

Key:

⟶⟶⟶⟶   Percentile points paired with Standard scale points.
– – – – –   Pupil at 78th percentile given 73 points on Standard Scale.

('bunchings' of pupils, for example) in the score distributions produced by different teachers. This method might suit those occasions when two or more sets take 'the same subject' but their courses are pitched at different levels and a common examination is not entirely appropriate. Separate examinations would produce marks and ranks within sets, then all pupils would be ranked together by overlapping sets, as judged by the teachers involved.

The effort required to carry out such procedures might only be justified at certain points in pupils' careers, such as option choice, examination guidance, band or set changes. Computer programs can be written to make the calculations for standard scales an easy matter. Several schools had done this and published programs are now being produced (see, for example, Cohen L. and Holliday M. (1982)). For schools in our sample who are trying computer scaling of marks, a major problem has been the provision of access time to enter raw scores on the computer file.

Grading procedures

It is common to compare a pupil's performance with those of others in the group and to award a grade accordingly. Problems arise, however, when comparisons of grades are made between groups; for instance, in assuming that Grade A in one set means the same level of attainment as in another.

Many schools use number or letter grades which relate to fixed proportions of pupil groups. A common system divides pupils' scores into five sections, as shown in Table 20.

Table 20: Five-point grading scheme

Grade	A	B	C	D	E
Percentage of group	10%	20%	40%	20%	10%

Our survey revealed many grading schemes, usually employing five grades but with different proportions of children assigned to each. This practice was typically described as 'grading on the normal curve' – a phrase used to justify its assumed technical adequacy. It illustrated widespread misunderstandings, however. One of these concerned the quality of performance being graded and how it might change across a group of pupils. If the quality of performance can be measured in finely graded steps (e.g., by awarding examination marks out of 100 per cent), development may be envisaged as cumulative and percentages awarded are points representing more or less attainment. On the other hand, if the quality is such that it can be measured in distinct stages (e.g., making five, ten, fifteen, etc. typing errors) or successive steps (e.g., 'observing and recording an experiment' followed by 'interpreting the data') any measurement ought to reflect steps between levels.

Grades applied to such a discontinuous scale i.e., to stepped levels, can only refer to specific performance criteria. Whatever the distribution of grades which results, even if the balance is lop-sided on either side of a 'middle' grade, there is no question of relating to a normal distribution. When the underlying scale is presumed to be continuous, however, and the distribution is taken to be bell-shaped, grading could be done 'on the normal curve', or approximately so.

If marks were awarded with a frequency distribution close to the normal then the size of the mark bands relating to each grade could vary widely. Figure 6 shows an example of how the mark bands vary from each grade division when the frequencies of marks awarded are as would be expected on a normal distribution. In this case the score is set at 100, and the SD at 15.

Figure 6: Grades and mark bands on a normal distribution

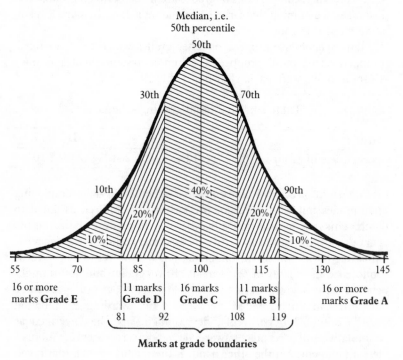

Marks at grade boundaries

Here the grades are distributed on a 10 per cent, 20 per cent, 40 per cent, 20 per cent and 10 per cent allocation scheme. Note that most of the extreme groups of pupils fall into groups labelled A or E but that 55 and 145 are not the respective lower and upper limits of the scale. Everyone within the middle 16 mark band is treated as a C grade, but 40 per cent of pupils are within this band. Then 11 marks are available for the next 20 per cent each way.

Table 21: Grade schemes

(a) for equal band widths

Grade	A	B	C	D	E
Group proportions	12%	22.5%	31%	22.5%	12%
Mark band width (approximate)	more than 12	12	12	12	more than 12

(b) for equal group proportions

Grade	A	B	C	D	E
Group proportions	20%	20%	20%	20%	20%
Mark band width (approximate)	more than 18	8	8	8	more than 18

When the three middle mark bands are made the same size the proportions are given in Table 21(a). However, using another scheme, equal proportions for each grade could be chosen to give mark band widths as shown in Table 21(b). We can see that any grading scheme which is 'balanced' and related to a normal distribution will have two extreme grades which have theoretically unlimited scores within the band (though we can specify the range within which most of the 'extreme' pupils will appear). Clearly, careful thought is needed to decide what 'a grade' is supposed to mean. If equal steps are supposed to be reflected by the distance between the boundaries of the grades then the distribution shown in Table 21(a) is the one to choose. This could be simplified without too much distortion of underlying scale values to 11 per cent, 22 per cent, 33 per cent, 22 per cent and 11 per cent – easily remembered proportions.

Error in mark scales and grade scales

Marks and grades, however scaled, are best regarded as approximate indicators. Standardized test manuals often show how 'test reliability' (i.e., the consistency of pupils' responses throughout the test, or the degree of correspondence between first and second attempts when pupils were re-tested, has been calculated). The 'standard error' value which results is then reflected in the size of the score bands within which the pupil's score would most frequently occur if re-tested repeatedly. These are referred to as confidence bands, which can then be determined.

Some common confidence bands are:

at the 68 per cent level (i.e., plus and minus one normal curve SD);
at the 95 per cent level (i.e., plus and minus two normal curve SDs);
at the 99 per cent level (i.e., plus and minus three normal curve SDs).

The respective factors of 1, 2 and 3 are applied to the 'standard error of score' value, more usually called the 'standard error of measurement' (or SEm). For example, if the SEm on a certain scale is calculated as 3.5 points, the associated confidence bands would be:

at 68 per cent – any pupil's score ± 3.5;
at 95 per cent – any pupil's score ± 7.0;
at 99 per cent – any pupil's score ± 10.5.

On the standardized test scale commonly used in Britain, i.e., mean set at 100, SD set at 15, (and for tests with reliabilities of a high order, e.g. of about 0.94 or above) the pupil's 'true' test score at the 95 per cent level of confidence would be most likely to lie in a band 14 points wide, with his obtained score at the middle. There would be a 5 per cent chance that this band would be too narrow; in other words, that the pupil's 'true' performance would have produced a score above the upper limit or below the lower limit. For 95 pupils out of 100 this would not be the case.

The SEm instanced above is typical of standardized tests. These usually have high reliabilities. School examinations have also been shown to have quite high reliabilities (but variations in applying mark schemes, e.g., by giving poorer pupils a few bonus points to encourage effort, reduce consistency). Take as an example a school examination marked out of 100 which is transposed to a scale with a mean of 50 and SD of 20. A standard error of about one quarter of the SD would be 5 points. The three confidence bands would be 10, 20 and 30 points wide.

Using the smallest band of 68 per cent (i.e., about ⅔ probability that the 'true' score is within the band), examination marks in two subjects less than five points apart would best be regarded as equivalent. For instance, a three subject profile might appear as in Figure 7.

Figure 7: A three subject profile

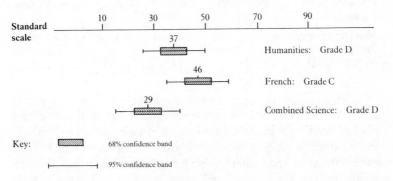

In this example, humanities overlaps the other subjects; only French and combined science can be regarded as sufficiently different to warrant taking a firm decision, such as a change of courses, based on these scores.

This example can be used to look at grade differences. Taking the scheme with 40 per cent of pupils assigned to grade C, only French would be classified so. The other two subjects would both fall into Grade D. We can see now how the use of marks or the use of grades could lead to widely disparate views about the pupil's progress. With the grade scheme, French is placed distinctively ahead of the other two subjects while, using the mark scheme, French is clearly distinguishable from combined science but not from humanities.

A large number of grades would offer more precision. In standardized testing, nine divisions equal to half of a standard deviation are often used (these 'stanines', for highly reliable tests only, have a standard error of about one stanine). However, a compromise between five and nine divisions is seven. This would also be more in line with the reliabilities associated with the assessments which underlie the grades. A further point, though not one which particularly commends the use of a seven grade scheme, is that it lines up quite well with a notional scale which combines 'O' level and CSE grades. Validating school predictions, as we have advocated, would be facilitated by using schemes which correspond in some respects.

Table 22: A seven grade scheme

Grade	G	F	E	D	C	B	A
Group proportions	5%	10%	20%	30%	20%	10%	5%
Mark band width for scale with Mean 100, SD 15	more than 10	10	10	10	10	10	more than 10
Mark band width for scale with Mean 50, SD 20	more than 14	13	13	14	13	13	more than 14

Table 22 gives the approximations for the percentages of pupils and score bands for a seven grade scheme. It has been shown that grades, being broad classifications, cannot be handled as readily as scores, from the standpoint of standard error of measurement. For examinations or tests where steps have been taken to ensure high reliability, the appropriate confidence band on a five grade scale would be plus or minus a half grade (at the 95 per cent level). It would be plus or minus $7/10$ths of a grade for a scale with seven grades. For those school grading schemes which have not been studied for reliability (i.e., consistency of the grader with his own criteria, or consistency between graders, or relationship between marks distributions and grade boundaries), the confidence band is more likely to be a whole grade wide. These aspects are especially important when grades rather than attainment criteria are used to gauge pupils' progress. In particular, it has to be borne in mind that profiles based on subjective judgments, not cross-checked between teachers, might well be unreliable. Hence, the associated errors may be relatively large.

Additional reading

We have dealt only briefly with some technical aspects. The following are publications which teachers engaged in reviewing assessment methods might find helpful: diagnostic assessment in secondary schools (Black and Dockrell, 1980); pupil profiles (Goacher, 1983); reading tests (Vincent and Cresswell, 1983); reviews of tests used in education in U.K. (Levy and Goldstein, 1983); principles and general assessment issues (Rowntree, 1977); pupils' learning in science (Harlen, 1983); assessment theory and practice including statistics (Satterly, 1981); issues and techniques relating to assessing secondary pupils (Deale, 1975; Black and Broadfoot, 1982). Full references to these appear in the back of the book. Additionally, there is a growing number of reports from the Assessment of Performance Unit's survey teams for mathematics, English, science and foreign languages, each of which features new methods.

(D) Pointers to good practice

In this section we make some specific suggestions for heads and teachers who are re-examining their school assessments. The checklists below are by no means definitive – the questions they raise are intended simply as a starting point for extension and adaptation within particular contexts (for example, detailed policy aims will vary according to subject, age of pupils etc.).

Throughout this report we have emphasized the necessity to focus first on the curriculum. Assessment schemes cannot be specified in a vacuum. The purposes, content and intended outcomes of the curriculum need to be set out in some detail – general statements are inadequate. Some teachers may be reluctant to adopt a 'behavioural objectives' approach because it chops up integrated learning outcomes and is unsuitable for higher learning aims. However, a possible compromise is to regard each year's work for a class as a course. In this there will be various types of activity, often organized in distinct, successive phases. One possible way to characterize these is in terms of knowledge and skills; for example, in science, knowing what to look for and how to make accurate observations using instruments. This kind of curriculum analysis is potentially much more useful than, for example, logging progress through a course as 'completed 39 out of 44 work cards', or clocking up weekly marks out of 10 for homework as a basis for awarding grades on a five-point scale.

Whether assessments have met the purposes intended can best be judged by examining the decisions or actions taken. It is for this reason that we suggest, in parallel with a number of assessment aims, some actions which may follow from their implementation. These actions will involve evaluation decisions about whether or not the aim has been met. Thus, a recurrent review of curriculum and its assessment is achieved. To take a simple example: allocations to 'O' level or CSE courses are made on the basis of predictions which can be checked against subsequent results (this particular follow-up will be affected by the exclusive allocations made and the partial overlap of courses). A relatively high 'failure' rate at 'O' level should at least prompt a re-think on allocation policy, for example.

Policy: its aims and their realization

A broad statement of aims might be:

> to produce accurate assessments of each pupil which relate to the work done in school courses, so that performance can be monitored and appropriate educational decisions reached in consultation with the pupil, parents and teachers.

The list below sets out selected assessment aims and, alongside, some examples of possible courses of action which may both result from the assessment and influence future assessments. We have divided them roughly into aims which involve corporate decisions (by the whole school, by departments, year group teachers etc.) and those which mainly concern the individual teacher in her classroom.

(i) ASSESSMENT AIMS FOR SCHOOLS/DEPARTMENTS, ETC.
(These lists are intended as exemplars only: they are not exhaustive.)

Aims	*Possible action taken/advice given*
(a) evaluate each pupil's attainment in English and mathematics on entry to the school	assign to bands/mixed ability groups; match pupils with curricula and vice versa
(b) appraise each pupil's verbal, symbolic and spatial abilities on entry to the school	provide appropriate extension learning activities for the individual
(c) rank order pupils on term exams	allocate to hierarchical teaching sets
(d) compare pupils within a year group	allocate to option groups
(e) appraise each course phase or module	record attainment on a course profile and examine patterns revealed in this profile

Aims	*Possible action taken/advice given*
(f) show each parent the standard attained by the pupil	improve interpretation of the results presented to parents; change pupil sets or change course contents
(g) assemble course performance data backed by standardized abilities tests data towards end of third secondary year	inform pupils and parents during guidance period prior to choosing examination courses
(h) describe certain behavioural and personality features	modify approaches in the pastoral care of the individual
(i) administer graded tests in particular subjects	award certificates
(j) award grades in line with external examining bodies within pupil ability bands	predict type of examination entry

(ii) ASSESSMENT AIMS FOR TEACHERS
(These lists are intended as exemplars only: they are not exhaustive.)

(k) give teacher feedback on the quality of learning in the class	adapt the curriculum, its pace, presentation, etc.
(l) indicate to each pupil his progress through the course	alternative teaching approaches, work habits or procedures recommended
(m) give feedback on effectiveness of learning on specific tasks	repeat task, vary learning experiences
(n) show teacher whether pupils understand the course objectives	explain/exemplify objectives to pupils
(o) identify individual learning difficulties and associated cognitive features	devise remedial learning experiences
(p) pre-test for graded objectives tests set externally	rehearse graded test procedures and choose pupils for entry

Implementing policies

Not all policy aims can be pursued with equal vigour at any one time; it may be preferable to tackle a few thoroughly. Below we offer a set of questions which are intended to clarify practical matters affecting the use of teachers' and pupils' time and other resources.

(i)   For each course, has an assessment specification been written down?

(ii)   Does the specification reflect the activities in the course, e.g., practicals, receptive/expressive products, projects, visits etc?

(iii)   Does the specification call for a range of methods, e.g., written examinations, oral tests, observations (ratings)?

(iv)   What is the timing of the assessments? Is the work load reasonable for pupils and teachers?

(v)   Who produced the assessment specification? Was it agreed as apt and practical by the teachers who use it?

(vi)   Has each course teacher got a copy?

(vii)   Do the teachers have all the skills required?

(viii)   Who will aggregate the marks, grades or ratings given? Who will collate the results from various components of the course? Are the technical methods satisfactory?

(ix)   What interpretations of results will be given to pupils? parents? to others (e.g., psychologist, attendance officer, social services, etc.)?

Reporting and recording

Here, the key question is interpretability. It is quite clear that unreliable data (i.e., scores likely to contain relatively large errors; grades awarded without defined criteria) will defy sensible interpretation. Hence, the first question:

(a)   Is the information on the record of known quality?

The major interested parties are well known, but the guidance they require to make sense of the record will vary. This is especially so when ostensibly the same scales are used for pupils deemed to belong to different levels of attainment or ability. So the next questions are:

(b)   Do the supporting documents give a clear explanation of the scheme to pupils, parents and others?

(c) How has understanding of the scheme been checked with pupils and parents?

Further questions might be:

(d) Does the scheme summarize the major components of course performance?

(e) Do departmental schemes supply data compatible with the school scheme?

(f) How does the scheme support educational and careers guidance?

(g) How does the system (scheme for recording, organization of reporting) help pupils to evaluate themselves at important decision points (e.g., changes of course, leaving school)?

(E) Summarizing remarks

In the development of policy we have suggested that attention should first focus on the purposes of assessment. Much time-consuming assessment goes on fairly unthinkingly, almost as a ritual, with little consideration given to why it is being carried out. It may be done for all kinds of 'weak' (and basically non-educational) reasons – such as that 'school policy dictates that all pupil work has to be marked' or 'the head of department requires twelve grades for each pupil by the end of term'. Too often these 'weak' reasons become ends in themselves. They lead nowhere. The results are not used for effective feedback to the pupil, for improvement of teaching or for revision of curricula. They become fossilized on a record card, a report form or a profile. Above all assessments should be designed so that they influence decision-making. It may be better, certainly more practicable, to select a small number of purposes to bear in mind when assessing a piece of work or a whole course.

Consideration of purposes will, it seems to us, almost inevitably lead to a more imaginative and thoughtful consideration of how pupils' work is evaluated, which aspects of that work can and should be assessed and who ought to be responsible for this assessment. A host of questions arise and guidance on many of these may be needed if assessment policies are to be translated into effective action. For example, it may be that formal assessments could usefully be supplemented by more 'informal' methods if these latter were made and recorded systematically. Teachers seem to believe that methods such as classroom observation of pupil activity, or their own reflections on the development of thinking in individual pupils are at least as valid as more 'objective' and 'scientific' methods. Research could usefully explore ways of thinking about and systematizing (but not invalidating) these less formal approaches to assessment. It may be that work other than set written pieces should be assessed – a pupil's oral contribution, his ability to listen, his attainment in practical activity and a variety of other aspects of performance may be just as important. Many teachers doubt whether they are in a position to assess pupils' personal attributes, such as initiative, honesty and integrity. Whether such assessments ought to be recorded for use by others is a matter for LEAs and perhaps for individual schools. It is the responsibility of the LEAs to support schools with in-service courses and other resources related to all these questions. Many teachers need guidance particularly on the technical problems associated with assessment.

It seems that written guidelines are useful and that assessments at school and departmental levels need coordination. The role of coordinator should be active and well-defined, aimed at resolving problems and encouraging developments by consultation. The post-holder needs to be technically informed. Comparability of marking and the scaling of scores will improve precision in awarding marks but even so they should be regarded as good approximations rather than exact values. Grades represent broad categories of pupils, though their use tends to obscure the question of probable misclassification (standard error of grading). Thought should be given to the interpretation of grade levels and the distinctions teachers make between adjacent grades when judging pupils subjectively. Complications are inherent when teaching sets are organized hierarchically and taught a different curriculum under the same subject label. Pupils may need to compare themselves with others or to compare their standing in different subjects. A departmental or school scheme which links sets and marks or grades might be helpful. It would need to be structured so that overlaps between sets, in attainment standards and course content, can be assessed in common. Microcomputer programs will offer teachers the facility to analyse examination results and, in addition, records from continuous and periodic assessments might be accumulated, combined and compared. Appropriate mixes of assessments, to provide the pupil data base, would need careful planning; computerized tests would have a place but written assessments, practicals and oral assessments should be given due prominence.

Perhaps assessment should be an activity done less to pupils and more with them. For example, an assessment scheme for a particular piece of work could be discussed with pupils. Too often the teacher may be clear on this, but pupils are in the dark about why the assessment is taking place and how it is to be carried out. Since the activity is being carried out ostensibly for their benefit, the meaning and value of assessment needs to be made plain to pupils. In addition, it seems that teachers would have much to gain from allowing pupils to share sometimes the responsibility for assessment of their own learning. In this case the criteria for assessment would need to be made explicit to pupils. Others in the school, parents, governors, employers, etc. all need to interpret assessment results, especially if they are scaled or graded. It is the school's responsibility to provide appropriate guidance for this interpretation.

Suggestions made in this report need not involve more teacher time spent on assessment. Only assessment procedures which lead to reasonable work loads can be expected to be effective. For example, time could be saved if teachers adopted different marking strategies at different times. An interspersion of several rough impressionistic assessments (which can be done rapidly) with assessments involving detailed evaluation and feedback to individual pupils may be both more valuable and less time-consuming overall, than a routine 'even' pattern of marking. We believe that thoughtful practice could result in a lighter work load than much of the routine assessment of homework and classwork recognized by teachers as a chore with limited value.

The suggestions for improving practice in the preceding section are intended to reflect (a) the fact that good policies include consideration of purposes, (b) that procedures (which avoid technical error) should focus on the realization of policy aims and (c) that record systems should allow the evaluation of these aims. It is this evaluation which can then inform decisions about future change.

Appendix 1

The survey questionnaires

(a)   Headteacher questionnaire (n=97)

(b)   Head of department/Head of year questionnaire (n=223)

(c)   Teacher questionnaire (n=460)

Results (in italics) have been added to the questionnaires to give an idea of the global response. For most questions the percentages given are of the total number of questionnaire respondents (see above). However, sometimes the context of the question required a different basis for calculation. For example, some results are given as percentages of respondents answering that particular item (and therefore they add up to 100 percent). Results for questions linked to a preceding question are obviously calculated as percentages of those answering the first question positively. In all cases the method of calculation is either obvious or made explicit in the Appendix.

Salient results of open-ended questions are summarized briefly, usually without percentage figures.

Results figures which appear in the text are sometimes calculated on a different basis (e.g., from a sub-sample of teachers using comparisons of answers to two or more questions by cross-tabulation). In all cases, however, this is made clear.

ASSESSMENT PROCEDURES IN SCHOOLS
for pupils aged 11–14
Questionnaire for Headteachers

Confidential

The purpose of this questionnaire is to obtain an accurate picture of current assessment practices in schools dealing with children within the 11 to 14 age range. All questions need therefore to be answered in terms of your arrangements for this age group.

We are aware of the fact that some schools may be in the process of developing an assessment policy and that in these cases all aspects of that policy will not yet have been decided upon. Your answers should, however, reflect the practices still in effect at the present time. However, if your school is in a transitional stage, the additional information sections provided at the bottom of each page may be used, where necessary, to indicate this.

Please respond to **every one** of the pre-coded questions **by circling a number.** In many cases individual practices are too complex to be answered in this way and, therefore, some questions ask for a written response.

Please include any documentation which you feel clarifies your assessment procedures. **All information you give will be treated in the strictest confidence.**

Section I

Policy

Please circle

1 Is there a written assessment policy for the whole school?

  YES NO
  47% 51%

2 (a) Is an assessment policy being developed at the moment?

  49% 44%

  (b) If yes, please indicate for how long you have been engaged in this development

less than 3 months	4–11 months	1yr–2yr	2yr–3yr	3 years
21%	25%	38%	10%	4%

3 Are there separate written assessment policies for each age group in the school?

  24% 74%

4 Are there separate written assessment policies for some department/subject areas in the school?
If yes – please give details.

  55% 41%

All departments in the school (11%). The most commonly

mentioned individual departments were mathematics

(21%), science (13%), modern languages (13%), and

English (10%)

Additional information

5 (a) In this question we wish to know in more detail about which staff were involved in originating the policies mentioned in Question 4.

Please indicate by circling which post holders made contributions to a policy or policies.

		School policy	All Depts/ year group/ subject area policies	Some Depts/ year group/ subject area policies	Own Depts/ year group/ subject area policies
i)	Head	68%	24%	10%	7%
ii)	Deputy head(s)	60%	23%	7%	10%
iii)	Senior teachers	32%	10%	2%	5%
iv)	Heads of years	41%	12%	11%	12%
v)	Heads of departments	45%	22%	16%	43%
vi)	Other teachers	33%	13%	13%	33%
vii)	Others please specify	4%	1%	2%	0%

(b) Please specify the heads of departments who were involved in originating policies in departments other than their own.

Several comments indicating involvement mainly of

academic and remedial departments

Please circle
YES   NO

6 (a) Does the assessment policy assume that some subjects or curriculum areas are inherently more difficult to assess than others?   61%   32%

Additional information

NFER
use
Card 1

(b) If yes, which subjects were considered more difficult?

i)	Aesthetic subjects	*52%*
ii)	Craft and technical subjects	*25%*
iii)	English	*7%*
iv)	Humanities...........................	*16%*
v)	Mathematics	*0%*
vi)	Modern languages.....................	*3%*
vii)	Physical education.....................	*35%*
viii)	Remedial education	*8%*
ix)	Science	*6%*
x)	Social/community studies	*20%*
xi)	Others	*1%*

please specify

Please circle
YES   NO

7 Has the school policy on assessment for the 11–14 year age group been influenced by the demands of the public examination system at 16+ years?   *54%   46%*

If so, please specify

24% of Middle Schools use public examination criteria.

Most secondary schools use public examination criteria at

age 13+

8 Has the school policy been influenced by LEA assessment practice (e.g. an LEA requirement to administer certain tests?)   *10%   90%*
If so, please give details

This includes standardized tests, some provided by LEA

mainly to entry groups; also graded modern language tests.

Additional information

NFER
use
Card

Please circle
YES   NO

9   Was any advice or information provided by
    LEA advisers in formulating the policy?   22%   78%
    If so, please give details
    Little by way of specific recommendations; some discussion

    in individual schools, focussed mainly in particular subject

    areas.

10 (a) Is your school involved in any local liaison
         scheme to provide pupil profiles for
         employers?   13%   87%

    (b) If so, has this scheme influenced the school
         assessment policy for the 11–14 year age
         group?   23%   67%

11 (a) Which of the following methods were
         used in formulating the school
         assessment policy?

                               (more than one may be circled)
    i)   Working parties of teachers   47%
    ii)   Working parties of senior staff   62%
    iii) Whole staff meetings   52%
    iv)   Individuals working alone   22%
    v)   Discussion papers   32%

    Please give details of origin and circulation
    Some introductory papers drawn up by head or senior

    member of staff, otherwise summary papers following

    discussion and meetings.

Additional information

NFER
use
Card 1

b)   Please comment as to the effectiveness of the various
     means which you employed

     The majority stressed the effectiveness of teacher

     consultations.

	Please circle
	YES NO

12   Are there any formal means whereby the
     current assessment policy for the school can be
     reviewed?   *64%   32%*
     If yes, please give details.

     Periodic meetings where policy is reviewed;

     otherwise senior staff or general staff

     meetings at which policy issues can be raised.

13   Have the school governors had any influence
     on the assessment policy?   *6%   94%*

14   If no to Q.13, how has the school assessment
     policy been communicated to the school
     governors?

     Headmasters' reports at Governors' meetings most

     common.

Additional information

Section II

The Scope of the Assessment Policy

The questions below are designed to allow a description of the assessment scheme used with the 11–14-year-olds in your school. If further information needs to be added please use the additional information space, or attach extra sheets or relevant documentation.

	Please circle YES	NO

15 Does the policy deal with the following aspects of assessment?

(a) A system of grading work 64%   29%

(b) A system of assessments relating performance of individuals to performance of a whole year group 85%   11%

(c) A system of assessments relating performances of individuals to performance in their group or set 71%   23%

(d) A system of assessments relating performances to individuals' own past performances 51%   39%

(e) A system of awarding marks or ratings or grades for effort 76%   20%

   If yes, please give details

Typically, five-point scales or five-letter grades.

(f) A system of standardizing marks in order, for example, to compare performances in different subjects and across different years 26%   71%

   If yes, please give details

Few used any scaling techniques or gave

instructions on mark distributions.

Additional information

NFER
use
Card 1

Please circle
YES   NO

(g) A system for combining continuous
assessments with periodic
assessments 49%   46%
If yes, please give details

Most answers show separate recording; minority

indicated combining to give grades A-E.

(h) A system of record keeping............. 92%   4%
If yes, please give details

Comprehensive range of individual and departmental

procedures given, including record cards and

computerized systems.

16 Does the assessment policy for the school
recognize achievement with prizes of any
kind?   43%   55%

If yes, please give details

Awarded usually for 'merit' or for exceptional effort

(certificates or books presented).

17 Does the school policy include liaison on
assessment with your contributing and
receiving schools?   82%   16%

If so, please give details

Typically involves transfer of test results; little evidence

of regular and close liaison.

18 Is a member of staff designated as
coordinator of assessment?   39%   58%

If yes, please give post

Deputy head (often responsible for curriculum

development) the most common; a few posts

designated for assessment.

Additional information

19 Which of the following assessment results
are included in a centralized record
keeping system?

(more than one may be circled)

(a) Results of diagnostic tests 71%
(b) Results of objectively marked tests
(multiple choice, etc.) 40%
(c) Results of continuous assessment 53%
(d) Results of informal teacher tests 17%
(e) Results of structured observations of
pupil performance 26%
(f) Results of self-assessment by pupils 6%
(g) Results of informal teacher assessments
of personal and attitudinal
characteristics 60%
(h) Results of published tests of personality 4%
(i) Results of published diagnostic tests 45%
(j) Results of published tests of attainment 37%
(k) Results of written essay-type
examinations 47%
(l) Results of speaking tests 8%
(m) Results of listening tests 9%
(n) Results of conversation tests 6%
(o) Results of projects 12%
(p) Results of course-work essays 12%
(q) Results of assessment of practical work 34%

Please circle
YES   NO

20 Are any marks used in the centralized record
keeping system standardized?   35%   61%

If yes, please give details

Referred mainly to results from standardized

(published) tests.

Additional information

21 What use is made of these records?

(more than one may be circled)

(a) School reports to parents *84%*

(b) Information to other teachers within
school................................ *86%*

(c) Information to other schools *79%*

(d) Other *23%*

Please specify

Entered on long-term record for possible future reference.

22 Who is authorized to have direct access to records?

	Records of marks	Records of health	Records of behaviour
(a) Teachers	*89%*	*65%*	*78%*
(b) Heads of departments	*72%*	*47%*	*63%*
(c) Senior teachers	*64%*	*52%*	*59%*
(d) Year group tutors	*65%*	*51%*	*61%*
(e) Heads of year	*70%*	*62%*	*71%*
(f) Deputies	*78%*	*70%*	*75%*
(g) Heads of schools to which pupils will be transferred	*60%*	*51%*	*55%*

23 If some teachers do not have direct access please indicate
how access to records is mediated

Typically through senior staff.

Additional information

Please circle
YES   NO

24 Are parents allowed access to school records
relating to their children other than through
reports?   37%   62%

If yes, please give details

Limited access available arising from individual

requests.

25 For how many complete years has the present
assessment policy been in operation?

less than one year	1–3 years	4–5 years	6–7 years	8–9 years	10+ years
7%	27%	23%	15%	10%	18%

Additional information

Section III

Implementation of Policy

Please circle
(more than one
may be circled)

26 Please indicate if any of the following
means are used to communicate the
assessment policy to the teaching staff

   (a) Written scheme issued to all members
of staff *42%*

   (b) Regular meetings to review or discuss
principles and practice (after school
hours) *75%*

   (c) Regular meetings to review or discuss
principles and practice (during school
hours) *28%*

   (d) Meetings with new members of staff
to discuss policy and practice *57%*

   (e) Other means........................   *11%*

   Please specify

Informal meetings and ad hoc discussions most common.

Please circle
YES   NO

27 Is any member of staff designated as a
coordinator of assessment practices
between departments, year groups or
subject areas?   *34%   65%*

If yes, please state the position this person holds

Usually deputy head or senior post holder.

Additional information

Please circle
YES   NO

28 Are there any other procedures so far not
    mentioned whereby coordination of
    assessment is attempted?   *12%*   *77%*

    If yes, please describe the procedure

    Mention of involvement of pastoral care staff most

    common.

Section IV

Changes

29 Please give details of any changes you are considering
    making in the system of assessment in the near future

    The need to coordinate and formalize assessment in the

    school and to improve the record system. Introduction

    of pupil profiles and diagnostic tests. Some responses

    focused on improvements needed at school transfer.

30 What are the major constraints on any improvements you
    would like to make in your assessment scheme? Please
    give details

    Time, lack of teacher expertise in assessment techniques

    and staff conservatism were most commonly mentioned.

Additional information

Section V

School Details

To assist with the analysis of this data we would be most grateful if you would provide us with the following school and biographical details

31 Name of school _____

32 Type of school _____

33 Number of staff _____

34 Number of pupils _____

35 Age range of pupils _____

Section VI

Biographical Details

36 Please circle the number that corresponds with your age group

20–25 years	26–30 years	31–35 years	36–40 years	41–45 years	46–50 years	51–60 years	60+ years
0	0	2%	13%	19%	18%	44%	4%

37 Please indicate the approximate number of full years you have been headmaster/headmistress

Please circle the code number below the category which includes your length of experience

0–3 years	4–6 years	7–10 years	11–15 years	16–20 years	21–25 years	26–30 years	31–35 years	36+ years
26%	18%	21%	14%	12%	6%	2%	1%	0

Additional information

38   Please indicate the number of full years you have been Head of your present school.

Please circle the code number below the category which includes your length of experience

0–3 years	4–6 years	7–10 years	11–15 years	16–20 years	21–25 years	26–30 years	31–35 years	36+ years
31%	21%	26%	17%	5%	0	0	0	0

39   Which of the following qualifications do you hold?   Please circle

Certificate of Education. 52%
BEd   0
BA/BSc etc. 56%
PGCE 34%
Masters Degree 25%
PhD   0
Other (please specify) 19%

40   Please circle the number that corresponds to the age group(s) of children which you teach at present

11–12 years	12–13 years	13–14 years
39%	31%	21%

Additional information

ASSESSMENT PROCEDURES IN SCHOOLS
for pupils aged 11–14

Questionnaire for Heads of Departments Heads of Year Groups Holders of Posts of Special Responsibility

Confidential

This questionnaire is intended to investigate the assessment policies and practices which apply to pupils of **11 to 14 years of age.** Please answer all questions in terms of your arrangements for this age group.

We would like to emphasise that by 'assessment' we include the less formal day-to-day assessment which is practised routinely in classrooms, as well as the more formal kinds such as school examinations, test batteries etc.

Some questions are pre-coded for ease of response, but in many cases certain practices are too complex to be dealt with in this way, and therefore some questions ask for a written response.

Please include any documentation you feel further clarifies your assessment procedures.

All responses made to, and documents included with, this questionnaire will be seen only by project staff and will be treated with complete confidence.

Please Note:

If you organize, coordinate, or are in any way responsible for some area of school activities, whether this is recognized by extra payment or not, we would wish you to respond to this questionnaire. It has not been possible, however, to refer to all the many titles and arrangements that exist in middle and secondary schools without making each question cumbersome. 'Department' has therefore been used throughout to include all those categories mentioned in question 1(a) below.

Section I

Assessment Policy

1 (a) Please indicate your kind of responsibility by circling the appropriate code number. Should you not find a category that describes your area of responsibility, please enter this in the space marked 'other'.

	Please circle
Head of department	*66%*
Teacher in charge of subject area...........	*17%*
Head of year.............................	*13%*
Post of special responsibility	*5%*
Other	*6%*

	Please circle	
	YES	NO
(b) Is there an agreed set of teaching aims within your department? (If you have a written statement of aims we would be most grateful if you could include this document with this questionnaire).	*88%*	*10%*
2 Does everyone concerned with the department accept an agreed set of assessment procedures?	*83%*	*15%*
3 Is there a document describing these agreed procedures and the related policy? (If so, we would be grateful if you would enclose a copy with this questionnaire).	*28%*	*69%*
4 Does the assessment policy cover and specify		
(a) the methods to be used by teachers in making assessments?	*66%*	*23%*
(b) the system of marks or grades awarded to pupils?	*70%*	*19%*
(c) periodic critical discussion of the operation of the system?	*60%*	*29%*
(d) methods whereby you, as person responsible, collect and collate results from teachers?	*61%*	*28%*

Please circle
YES   NO

(e) ways in which information from
assessment is fed back to departmental
reviews of curricular content and
teaching methods?   42%   44%

(f) guidance for teachers about giving
advice to pupils on their performance as
well as their marks or grades?   30%   56%

5 If there is an agreed assessment policy,
please indicate which post holders were
involved in drawing it up. (Do not include an
individual more than once).

	YES	NO
(a) Head of this department	71%	3%
(b) Headteacher	24%	19%
(c) Deputy headteacher(s)	20%	20%
(d) Other heads of department	17%	20%
(e) Second in the department	25%	16%
(f) Teachers in the department	50%	10%
(g) Other teachers	8%	24%

6 Do you ensure that a new teacher involved
with your department is made aware of the
assessment policy?   72%   7%

If yes, please specify how this is done

More than half the responses mentioned discussion or

explanation. The next most common methods were

printed information sheets and exercises involving

moderation of pupils' work.

7 Are your departmental assessment practices
determined at all by the school's assessment
policy?   55%   39%

If so, please say how

General school assessment policy influenced departments;

the most common pattern being a standardized school

grading system. Others mentioned common year-group

examinations.

Please circle
YES   NO

8 (a) Is there someone in overall charge of
       coordination of assessment in your
       school?   39%   58%
  (b) If so, please indicate what kind of help or
       advice you have received from him/her.

Most mentioned translation of marks into school grading

systems. Others noted meetings and discussions and help

with statistical procedures.

9 Do you have curricular links with other
   departments within the school (e.g. inter-
   departmental agreements on an order of
   presenting certain topics)? If so, please give
   details. If no, move to Question 11.   40%   57%

Links with mathematics and English departments were

most common. A few mentioned links through 'topic' or

theme work.

10 If yes to Question 9 – are your curricular links
   with other departments accompanied by
   links in assessment procedures?   10%   37%
   If so, please specify

Of the few responses most mentioned common grading

schemes.

11 (a) Is a proportion of the homework set in
       your department meant to receive
       marks?   56%   33%
   (b) If yes, please indicate how much

less than 10%	11–30%	31–50%	51–70%	71–90%	more than 90%
4%	5%	14%	18%	20%	38%

NFER use

(c) Would you estimate what proportion of homework actually does receive marks

less than 10%	11–30%	31–50%	51–70%	71–90%	more than 90%
4%	7%	17%	19%	19%	35%

Section II

Methods and Uses of Assessment

12 What are the main methods (e.g. written examinations, objectively marked tests, practical examinations) employed in your department for assessments which are recorded? Please give details

Written examinations recorded much more frequently

than other assessments, followed by objective tests and

practicals. Continuous assessment, homework, oral work

etc. noted much less frequently.

Please circle

	YES	NO

13 Do you use published tests? 24% 71%

If yes, please give details of titles

Forty tests mentioned. Those most quoted were Daniels

and Diack, Neale Analysis, Non-verbal reasoning test,

NFER Mathematics, Richmond tests, Schonell.

Card 4

14 (a) Are all or almost all pupils within some year groups given a common examination or teachers' rating at some time? 87% 8%

(b) Please indicate how often and when

	Once every year	Twice every year	Three times every year	More often
11–12 year olds	34%	14%	9%	12%
Specify month(s)				

12–13 year olds	35%	14%	9%	11%
Specify month(s)				
13–14 year olds	35%	21%	10%	10%
Specify month(s)				

14 (c) Please indicate which groups of pupils are set examinations not taken by other groups

	11–12	12–13	13–14
All sets or bands have own examinations	21%	23%	24%
Low sets or bands	3%	4%	8%
High sets or bands	2%	3%	9%
Remedial sets or bands	13%	13%	16%
Others	4%	4%	4%

Please circle

	YES	NO
(d) Please indicate who sets the examinations mentioned in 14(c)		
(i) Teachers contribute questions	60%	3%
(ii) Head of department contributes questions	51%	4%
(iii) Other arrangements	7%	12%
(e) Please indicate whether grades or marks used in the examinations mentioned in 14(c) are chosen:		
(i) Individually by teachers	15%	18%
(ii) Departmentally	48%	7%
(iii) As part of school policy	28%	11%
15 (a) Are any predictions about performance in examinations at 16+ made on the basis of those mentioned in Q13?	29%	54%

NFER
use
Card 4

(b) If yes, in which age group are the
predictions made?

Please circle

11–12 year olds	*2%*
12–13 year olds	*12%*
13–14 year olds	*98%*

(c) To what use are the predictions put?

(i) Allocation of pupils to CSE/'O' level — *100%*

(ii) Allocation of pupils to non-examination group — *54%*

(d) Do you chart or correlate pupil external
examinations results with the records of
any results obtained during the

	YES	NO
11–14 years period?	*4%*	*49%*
14–16 years period?	*23%*	*33%*

16 (a) Are some methods of assessment used
in your department chosen to conform
with those used in public examinations? *47%* *39%*

(b) If yes to the above, to which age group(s)
are they applied?

	11–12	12–13	13–14
High sets or bands	*18%*	*28%*	*82%*
Middle sets or bands	*18%*	*25%*	*73%*
Low sets or bands	*11%*	*15%*	*54%*
Remedial sets or bands	*5%*	*7%*	*28%*

17 What are the **main methods** employed in your department
for informal assessments (e.g. short teacher tests, pupil
self-assessment)?

Please give details

Tests were by far the most common method, followed by

continuous assessment and a combination of classwork and

homework. A few mentioned observation and pupil

self-assessment.

NFE use Card

Please circle
YES   NO

18 (a) Do all members of your department use the same marking/grading system?   68%   26%

(b) Please describe the system, or systems used

Most commonly a five-point scale of ability (sometimes

incorporating the notion of balanced distribution) was used.

Marks out of predetermined totals and grades allocated to

continuous assessment were also mentioned.

19 (a) Do you collect assessment results from the teachers in your department or concerned with your area of responsibility? If NO please move to question 20.   67%   29%

If YES to (a)

(b) Do you combine the results into an aggregated or summary record for each pupil (i.e. marks or grades, etc.)?   77%

(c) Are these records used for any of the following purposes?

	A lot (80–100% of pupils)	A little (30–79% of pupils)	Hardly ever (10–29% of pupils)	Seldom (less than 10% of pupils)
(i) Allocation of pupils to sets or groups	54%	15%	2%	14%
(ii) Deciding how to help individual pupils	32%	27%	8%	21%
(iii) Reviewing departmental schemes of work	28%	21%	7%	21%
(iv) Reviewing pupil performance overall as a means of assessing the effectiveness of departmental teaching	33%	17%	7%	21%
(v) Giving pupils a clear indication of their progress in a year group	62%	11%	5%	10%

NFER
use
Card 4

20 Are the assessment results used by teachers as follows:

	A lot (80–100% of pupils)	A little (30–79% of pupils)	Hardly ever (10–29% of pupils)	Seldom (less than 10% of pupils)
(i) Allocation of pupils to sets or groups	61%	19%	4%	18%
(ii) Deciding how to help individual pupils	54%	28%	10%	17%
(iii) Reviewing departmental schemes of work	36%	23%	10%	24%
(iv) Reviewing pupil performance overall as a means of assessing the effectiveness of departmental teaching	40%	27%	10%	23%
(v) Giving pupils clear indications about progress in a teaching set	70%	15%	6%	12%

Please circle
YES NO

21 Are any of the following statistical procedures applied to your departmental results?

	YES	NO
(a) Calculation of means	25%	62%
(b) Graphs of distribution	29%	58%
(c) Standard deviations	13%	72%
(d) Classification of pupils in score bands	31%	53%
(e) Comparison of means for two or more different assessments	13%	70%
(f) Transformation of raw scores to another scale	27%	58%
(g) Analysis of individual questions (e.g. per cent correct)	23%	63%

Card 5

22 (a) Do you make use of the following technical equipment in processing your assessment results?

	YES	NO
(i) Computers	5%	86%
(ii) Microprocessors	1%	86%
(iii) Pocket calculator	43%	51%

NFE
use
Card

(b) If so, have you received any technical advice or training in the use of this equipment or any other techniques?

Please specify

The few responses indicated attendance on computer

courses and other LEA or DES in-service courses.

Please circle
YES   NO

23 Have you attended any in-service course(s) on assessment?   *23%   70%*

If so, please give details (e.g. date, course title, organizers of course, etc.)

Moderation meetings for examination boards were most

commonly mentioned.

24 If your assessment results are used for any other purpose than those specified above, either by you or anyone else, please give details

Few other purposes mentioned, mainly the giving of

information to other schools and to parents.

25 Can you give any examples of any action taken within your department (e.g. curricular changes, reorganization of pupil groupings, etc.) which has been taken on the basis of assessment results?

Of the large number of responses most mentioned some

form of pupil re-grouping; a number of others changed

course contents.

26 Please describe the scales of marks used in your
department (e.g. marks out of 5, 10, 100, etc.)

A variety of scales used (often several per department)

but percentages were the most common both for

classwork and examinations.

27 Please indicate which of the following attributes are
recognized in your assessment scheme, and how they
are recognized

	Marks given	Grades given	Ratings given
Application	18%	48%	16%
Progress	28%	46%	12%
Attitude	7%	46%	18%

28 Please indicate which records are received and (where
applicable) sent by you with children when they transfer
to or from your school

	Sent by you	Received by you
(a) The feeder school's own record card	17%	41%
(b) Samples of work by children	9%	15%
(c) Results of standardized tests	22%	34%
(d) Class or year lists of attainment	20%	17%
(e) Oral information from relevant staff	29%	40%
(f) The authority's official record card	22%	29%
(g) Teacher's grades of pupil's attitudes	27%	25%

NFE
use
Card

Please circle

		YES	NO

29 Please indicate if any of the following uses
    are made of reports received from feeder
    schools

		YES	NO
(a)	Used to form sets	25%	38%
(b)	Used to form streams or bands	24%	37%
(c)	Used to inform class tutors as background	57%	13%
(d)	Used to inform subject teachers as background	52%	17%
(e)	Other	5%	25%

Section III

Changes

30 If you think that the assessment presently carried out in your department could be improved could you list improvements in some order of priority and say roughly how long you think they would take to implement?

The need to establish a set of guidelines for marking

criteria and assessment procedures within and between

departments mentioned most often. Other responses

advocated more testing.

31 What would be the ideal mechanism for bringing about these changes (e.g. who would you like to involve etc.)?

Responses reflected recognition of importance of

consultation, either within departments or throughout

the school.

32 What are the main difficulties/impediments in putting these ideas into practice?

Time, lack of resources and the need to convince staff of

importance of assessment most frequently mentioned.

Section IV

Biographical Details

33 Please circle the number that corresponds with your age group

20–25 years	26–30 years	31–35 years	36–40 years	41–45 years	46–50 years	51–60 years	60+ years
0	*14%*	*31%*	*20%*	*14%*	*11%*	*10%*	*0*

34 Please circle the number which corresponds to your full years as a head of department/year group etc.

0–5	6–10	11–15	16–20	21–25	26–30	31–35	36–40	40+
33%	*30%*	*12%*	*12%*	*7%*	*2%*	*2%*	*1%*	*1%*

35 Please circle the number that corresponds to the number of full years in your present post

Less than 1	1–3	4–6	7–10	11–15	16–20	21–25	26–30	30+
8%	*23%*	*21%*	*21%*	*13%*	*9%*	*3%*	*2%*	*1%*

36 Please circle the number that corresponds to the age group(s) of children which you teach at present

Age 11–12 years	*58%*
Age 12–13 years	*65%*
Age 13–14 years	*73%*

Please circle

37 Which of the following qualifications do you hold?

Certificate of Education	*65%*
BEd	*13%*
BA/BSc etc	*36%*
PGCE	*20%*
Masters Degree	*3%*
PhD	*0*
Other	*8%*

Section V

NFER
use
Card 6

School Details

38 Name of school _____

39 Type of school _____

40 (a) Name of your department/area
        of responsibility _____

    (b) Number of staff for whom you
        have a coordination
        responsibility _____

Please use the following space for any further comments you
may wish to make:

ASSESSMENT PROCEDURES IN SCHOOLS
for pupils aged 11–14
Questionnaire for Teachers

Confidential

We would like your help in a project which is focusing on assessment procedures used in the early secondary years of schooling; that is, with pupils aged 11 to 14 years. The project is based in Sheffield and is concentrating its investigations in a group of northern authorities. Your school is taking part in the research and we are inviting all teachers to complete this questionnaire which seeks to discover the range of practices used by teachers in assessment across different areas of the curriculum. **We do not, of course, expect any one teacher's assessment practices to cover all the aspects mentioned.**

We would like to emphasize that by 'assessment' we include the less formal day-to-day assessment which is practised routinely in classrooms, as well as the more formal kinds such as school examinations, test batteries etc.

Space has been provided at the end for any additional information or comments you wish to make. **All information you give will be treated in the strictest confidence, and there is no need to write your name on the questionnaire.**

Please respond to every one of the pre-coded questions by circling a number.

Section I

Assessment Practices

Please answer all questions with reference to the 11–14 age group. Where no distinction is made, please refer to the general assessment situation.

The questionnaire is being distributed to both middle and secondary schools with a variety of organizational patterns. Some teachers may belong to a subject-based department or faculty, while others may teach as part of a year group team.

1 (a) Please indicate which of the following applies to you by circling the appropriate code number. Should you not find a category which describes your position please enter this in the space marked 'other'.

	Please circle
Teacher within a subject department	88%
Teacher within a year group	11%
Other	4%

	YES	NO
(b) Do you teach more than one subject	63%	36%

(c) Please indicate which subject(s) you teach and the approximate proportion of time spent on each by circling the appropriate code(s).

	25% time	25–50% time	50–75% time	75%+ time
Classteacher/general subjects teacher	32%	16%	11%	41%
Aesthetics and craft	16%	13%	10%	61%
Careers education	57%	38%	5%	0
Commerce and business studies	14%	0	14%	71%
English	29%	16%	8%	49%
Humanities other than English	35%	19%	9%	37%

NFE
use
Card

Mathematics	17% 19%	8% 57%
Modern and Classical languages	17% 10%	8% 65%
Physical education	20% 11% 13% 38%	
Remedial education	39% 13%	8% 39%
Sciences	21% 7%	5% 67%
Social/community studies	21% 7%	5% 67%

N.B. These have been calculated as row percentages – i.e. horizontally they add up to 100%

2   (a) Could you please indicate which marking or grading system(s) you use by circling the appropriate code

	Comment with no marks or grades		Grading system		Marks out of a pre-deter-mined total	
	*	†	*	†	*	†
Classteacher/general subjects teacher	6%	77%	5%	53%	4%	46%
Aesthetics and craft	5%	17%	11%	52%	11%	62%
Careers education	3%	0	0	0	0	0
Commerce and business studies	0	0	0	0	1%	0
English	11%	52%	13%	71%	10%	45%
Humanities other than English	7%	35%	12%	52%	14%	79%
Mathematics	7%	40%	8%	33%	18%	91%
Modern and Classical languages	3%	23%	5%	40%	10%	88%
Physical education	5%	53%	6%	70%	0	0
Remedial education	4%	66%	2%	53%	2%	40%
Sciences	6%	31%	9%	48%	14%	84%
Social/community studies	2%	100%	2%	50%	1%	50%

* Percentage responses from whole sample
† Percentage of responses from each department

If you use a different assessment system from the ones specified in the Table above, could you please give details below:

Responses mentioned combination of systems such as

grade with comment or effort grade with comment.

(It was of course quite possible for teachers to indicate

use of more than one system in the above table and many

did so.)

Please circle
YES   NO

(b) Do you have a preference for any of the
marking or grading systems used?   36%   53%

Please indicate which, with reasons if possible:

A third of the responses indicated a preference for marks

out of a predetermined total; fewer preferred grades and

comments.

If you do teach within a subject department or faculty but teach more than one subject could you please answer the remaining questions in the light of the subject you **mainly** teach.

3 Is there a written school policy relating to
assessment in this school?   40%   54%

4 Have you ever
(a) read it?   35%   25%
(b) discussed it with colleagues?   44%   19%
(c) been to a staff meeting where it was
discussed?   34%   62%

5 Is there a separate written policy in the
department or the year group in which you
teach?   30%   62%

NFE
use

Please circle
YES   NO

6   Were you included in the origination of this
policy?   20%   53%

7   Do you feel that either the school or the
departmental/year group policies give you
enough guidance in order to carry out the
assessment practices required of you?

School policy   44%   34%
Departmental/year group policy   63%   20%

Card

8   Do you use any of the following systems to
process marks?

(a) Recording marks in a way that shows
performance on different aspects of the
subject   68%   23%
(b) Changing marks to a different scale   37%   42%
(c) Combining marks from different tests   58%   26%
(d) Combining marks from different subjects   8%   69%
(e) Converting marks to grades   66%   21%
(f) Converting marks to percentages   62%   24%

9   If you graded or marked for attainment did
you compare performance in the main with:

(a) students' own work   63%   15%
(b) work done by others in the class   68%   9%
(c) work done by others in the band/stream   46%   22%
(d) work done by others in the year   54%   21%
(e) some other basis of comparison   4%   48%

10 If you feel that the assessment schemes you are using
could be altered in any way, please indicate by circling
the code number in the appropriate column. If you are
satisified with the methods you use please circle 5 in
each case.

	Introduce into the scheme		Make more use of the method	Make less use of or discard	Retain unchanged
	Yes	No			
(a) Informal teacher assessments	5%	2%	13%	2%	78%
(b) Informal teacher assessments of personal and attitudinal characteristics	5%	4%	20%	1%	70%
(c) Informal observations of pupil performance	5%	2%	16%	1%	76%
(d) Written examinations	1%	2%	7%	12%	78%
(e) Assessments of speaking	8%	14%	26%	3%	50%
(f) Assessments of listening	10%	10%	25%	3%	52%
(g) Assessments of conversation	9%	13%	25%	4%	49%
(h) Projects	8%	9%	17%	8%	59%
(i) Essays	2%	12%	8%	7%	71%
(j) Self-assessment by pupils	16%	16%	22%	7%	39%
(k) Use of diagnostic tests	9%	11%	17%	4%	59%
(l) Use of continuous assessment	5%	3%	23%	0	69%
(m) Use of grades rather than percentages	1%	7%	8%	7%	77%
(n) Use of percentages rather than grades	2%	13%	5%	13%	68%

(o) Standardization between departments	19% 11% 27% 4% 40%
(p) Standardization between markers in your department(s)	11% 2% 31% 0 55%
(q) Use of objectively marked tests (multiple choice, etc.)	8% 11% 16% 5% 61%
(r) Published tests of personality	6% 37% 5% 9% 43%
(s) Published diagnostic tests	11% 25% 9% 7% 48%
(t) Published tests of attainment	8% 21% 13% 7% 51%
(u) Structured observations of pupil performance	13% 10% 22% 2% 54%

N.B. These have been calculated as row percentages

11 (a) Referring to the list in question 10, please indicate those techniques you were involved in introducing for your department or school

Technique	a	b	c	d	e	f	g	h	i	j
Code (please circle)	4%	5%	4%	5%	2%	3%	2%	6%	2%	2%

Technique	k	l	m	n	o	p	q	r	s	t
Code (please circle)	2%	8%	3%	2%	2%	9%	7%	0	1%	2%

<table>
<tr><td></td><td></td><td></td><td></td><td></td><td></td></tr>
</table>

NFER
use
Card 9

*(b) Referring to the list in question 10, please indicate
those techniques you were involved in modifying and
developing for your department or school*

Technique	a	b	c	d	e	f	g	h	i	j
Code (please circle)	5%	4%	5%	17%	4%	3%	3%	6%	3%	2%

Technique	k	l	m	n	o	p	q	r	s	t
Code (please circle)	3%	11%	5%	2%	3%	14%	8%	0	0	1%

	Please circle	
	YES	NO
12 (a) Are there any aspects of pupil performance which you feel are inherently difficult to assess?	69%	14%

(b) If yes, do they include any of the
following?

	YES	NO
(i) Personality	50%	8%
(ii) Motivation	50%	13%
(iii) General ability	11%	28%
(iv) Creativity	40%	13%
(v) Spoken expression	24%	22%
(vi) Written expression	8%	29%
(vii) Other	5%	18%

Section II

NFER
use
Card 9

Uses of Assessment

	Please circle	
	YES	NO
13 Do you teach 11–12 year olds	*61%*	*20%*
12–13 year olds	*67%*	*18%*
13–14 year olds	*83%*	*6%*

Please answer Qs. 14–19 *only* for the years which you teach

	YES NO 11–12 (n=281)	YES NO 12–13 (n=308)	YES NO 13–14 (n=381)
14 Do you use assessments in order to create groups within the classes you teach, based on ability?	*20% 80%*	*16% 84%*	*18% 83%*
15 Do you use assessment results as the main method of giving feedback to your students?	*52% 49%*	*54% 47%*	*56% 45%*
16 Are your assessment methods designed to prepare children for external examinations later in their school careers?	*45% 56%*	*54% 47%*	*74% 27%*
17 Do you use your grades or marks as a prediction of the courses the students will follow into external examinations?	*34% 67%*	*44% 56%*	*76% 25%*
18 Do you test children regularly as a means of encouraging them to work hard?	*62% 39%*	*61% 40%*	*64% 37%*
19 Do you use your assessments as a means to judge the effectiveness of your teaching?	*77% 24%*	*73% 28%*	*77% 23%*

Section III

NFER
use
Card 9

Views on Assessment

20 We would like to gain your opinion as to the importance
you attach to the following styles of assessment. Please
reply so as to indicate **what you would prefer,** rather
than **what you do** at the present time.

Circling 1 would indicate that you feel such a method is
essential to gain a proper picture of a student. Circling 2
would indicate that you feel such a form of assessment is
important, but could be left out without distortion of the
student's ability. Circling 3 would indicate that you feel
this form of assessment is unnecessary.

		Essential	Important	Unnecessary
(a)	Regular examinations at least once per term	11%	31%	58%
(b)	Continuous assessment based on essay writing	13%	36%	51%
(c)	Examinations at the end of every year	57%	33%	11%
(d)	Making informal assessments of student's behaviour	47%	48%	5%
(e)	Including marks which show improvement or decline in a student's individual performance	52%	43%	5%
(f)	Using tests which show whether students have reached a predetermined standard	19%	52%	29%
(g)	Comparing marks or grades with other teachers to ensure agreement	34%	48%	18%
(h)	Assessing spoken expression	16%	58%	26%
(i)	Answering questions verbally	32%	60%	8%
(j)	Continuous assessment based on objective style tests	13%	56%	32%

(k) Assessments based on project
     work

| 9% | 46% | 46% |

(l) Continuous assessment based
     on classwork

| 50% | 43% | 6% |

(m) Marks or grades for effort
     included in assessments

| 57% | 38% | 5% |

(n) Assessments to enable
     comparison of students with
     national standards

| 12% | 47% | 41% |

(o) Self-assessments by students as
     part of an assessment scheme

| 8% | 42% | 50% |

(p) Diagnostic-type tests as part of
     an assessment scheme

| 13% | 48% | 40% |

*N.B. These have been
calculated as row
percentages*

Section IV

Background Information

21 Name of school _____

                                                 Please circle
22 Male   47%
    Female   53%

23 Full-time teacher   96%
    Part-time teacher   4%

24 Please circle the number that corresponds with your age
    group.

20–25 years	26–30 years	31–35 years	36–40 years	41–45 years	46–50 years	51–60 years	60+ years
18%	30%	23%	11%	6%	5%	6%	0

25 Please circle the number which corresponds to your full
years in teaching.

0–5	6–10	11–15	16–20	21–25	26–30	31–35	36–40	40+
40%	30%	14%	7%	3%	2%	3%	0	0

26 Please circle the number which corresponds to the
number of full years in your present school.

less than 1	1–3	4–6	7–10	11–15	16–20	21–25	26–30	30+
15%	31%	22%	18%	7%	4%	2%	0	0

27 Please circle the number that corresponds to the age
group(s) of children which you teach at present.

	Please circle
Age 11–12 years	63%
Age 12–13 years	70%
Age 13–14 years	86%

28 Which of the following qualifications do you hold?

Certificate of Education	59%
BEd	16%
BA/BSc etc.	39%
PGCE	27%
Masters Degree	4%
PhD	1%
Other (please specify)	4%

_____

_____

_____

Please use the following space for any further comments you
may wish to make:

References

BLACK, H.B. and BROADFOOT, P. (1982). *Keeping Track of Teaching*. London: Routledge & Kegan Paul.

BLACK, H.B. and DOCKRELL, W.B. (1980). *Diagnostic Assessment in Secondary Schools. A Teacher's Handbook*. Edinburgh: Scottish Council for Research in Education.

BUCKBY, M. (1980). *Graded Objectives and Tests for Modern Languages*. London: Schools Council.

COHEN, L. and HOLLIDAY, M. (1982). *Statistics for Social Scientists. Introductory Text with Computer Programs in BASIC*. London: Harper & Row.

DEALE, R. (1975). *Assessment and Testing in the Secondary School*. London: Evans/Methuen.

GOACHER, B. (1983). *Recording Achievement at 16+*. London Longman, for Schools Council.

GREAT BRITAIN. DEPARTMENT OF EDUCATION AND SCIENCE (1979). *Curriculum 11–16 working papers by H.M. Inspectorate: a contribution to current debate*. London: HMSO.

HARDING, A., PAGE, B. and ROWELL, S. (1980). *Graded Objectives in Modern Languages*. London: CILT.

HARLEN, W. (1983). *Guide to Assessment in Education: Science*. London: Macmillan Educational.

HARRISON, A. (1982). *Review of Graded Tests*. Schools Council Examinations Bulletin 41. London: Methuen Educational.

LEVY, P. and GOLDSTEIN, H. (1983). *Tests in Education*. London: Academic Press.

ROWNTREE, D. (1977). *Assessing Students: How shall we know them?* London: Harper & Row.

SATTERLY, D. (1981). *Assessment in Schools*. Oxford: Basil Blackwell.

STILLMAN, A. and MAYCHELL, K. (1984). *School to School: LEA and teacher involvement in educational continuity*. Windsor: NFER–NELSON.

WILCOX, B. (1982). 'School Self–Evaluation: the benefits of a more focused approach', *Educational Review*, 34, 3, 185–93.

VINCENT, D. and CRESSWELL, M. (1976). *Reading Tests in the Classroom*. Windsor: NFER–NELSON.